THE POLICE AND THE PUBLIC

Borgo Press Books by S. Fowler Wright

Arresting Delia: An Inspector Cleveland Classic Crime Novel
The Attic Murder: An Inspector Combridge & Mr. Jellipot Classic Crime Novel
The Bell Street Murders: An Inspector Combridge & Mr. Jellipot Classic Crime Novel
Beyond the Rim: A Lost Race Fantasy
Black Widow: A Classic Crime Novel
The Capone Caper: Mr. Jellipot vs. the King of Crime: A Classic Crime Novel
Crime & Co.: An Inspector Cleveland Classic Crime Novel
Dawn: A Novel of Global Warming
Dead by Saturday: An Inspector Cleveland Classic Crime Novel
Dream; or, The Simian Maid: A Fantasy of Prehistory (Marguerite Cranleigh #1)
Elfwin: An Historical Novel
The End of the Mildew Gang: An Inspector Cauldron Classic Crime Novel (Mildew Gang #3)
Four Callers in Razor Street: An Inspector Combridge & Mr. Jellipot Classic Crime Novel
The Hanging of Constance Hillier: An Inspector Cleveland Classic Crime Novel
The Hidden Tribe: A Lost Race Fantasy
The Jordans Murder: An Inspector Combridge & Mr. Jellipot Classic Crime Novel
The King Against Anne Bickerton: A Classic Crime Novel
The Mildew Gang: An Inspector Cauldron Classic Crime Novel (Mildew Gang #1)
Murder in Bethnal Square: An Inspector Combridge & Mr. Jellipot Classic Crime Novel
The Police and the Public: Some Thoughts on the British System of Justice
Post-Mortem Evidence: An Inspector Combridge & Mr. Jellipot Classic Crime Novel
The Return of the Mildew Gang: An Inspector Cauldron Classic Crime Novel (Mildew Gang #2)
The Rissole Mystery: An Inspector Combridge & Mr. Jellipot Classic Crime Novel
The Screaming Lake: A Lost Race Novel
The Secret of the Screen: An Inspector Combridge & Mr. Jellipot Classic Crime Novel
Spiders' War: A Novel of the Far Future (Marguerite Cranleigh #3)
Three Witnesses: A Classic Crime Novel
Too Much for Mr. Jellipot: An Inspector Combridge & Mr. Jellipot Classic Crime Novel
The Vengeance of Gwa: A Fantasy of Prehistory (Marguerite Cranleigh #2)
Was Murder Done? A Classic Crime Novel
Who Murdered Reynard? A Classic Crime Novel
The Wills of Jane Kanwhistle: An Inspector Combridge & Mr. Jellipot Classic Crime Novel
With Cause Enough?: An Inspector Combridge & Mr. Jellipot Classic Crime Novel

THE POLICE AND THE PUBLIC

Some Thoughts on the British System of Justice

by

S. Fowler Wright

The Borgo Press

An Imprint of Wildside Press LLC

MMIX

Copyright © 1929 by S. Fowler Wright
Copyright © 2009 by the Estate of S. Fowler Wright
Originally pubished under the title: *Police and Public*

All rights reserved.
No part of this book may be reproduced in any form
without the expressed written consent
of the author and publisher.
Printed in the United States of America

www.wildsidepress.com

FIRST WILDSIDE EDITION

CONTENTS

1. The Present Position 7
2. Police and Magistrate 12
3. Police Evidence 24
4. Corruption 32
5. The 'Voluntary' Statement 47
6. The Savidge Enquiry 60
7. The Smile of Inspector Collins 78
8. The Public Butler 90
9. The Staging of Murder Trials 116
10. Publicity 124
11. Conclusions 130

About the Author 138

"There are times and circumstances when not to speak out is at least to connive."

—EDMUND BURKE

The Police and the Public, by S. Fowler Wright

CHAPTER I.

The Present Position

It is an apparent necessity in any civilised state, unless it be one in which the whole body of citizens are of one mind in observing its laws, and in interpretation of mutual obligations, that there be some organised body of police to detect or restrain the activities of the insubordinate members of its population.

If the laws of a state be such as have the general support of its citizens, it should naturally follow that this police force will be regarded as a bulwark of social liberty, and will be generally popular.

This reflection is particularly applicable to the relations which should exist between the public and police of a 'democratic' state, the laws of which are (supposed to be) the expression of the common will of the community, and if there be a widespread feeling of distrust, or fear, or hostility, and there are unmistakable evidences of such feelings in England today, it becomes important to consider whether they arise from the nature of the laws which the police are required to administer, from the methods they adopt for such administration, from defects of integrity, or merely from misunderstanding and prejudice, such as may be removed by a frank enquiry.

If the evil exist, it is of the first importance that its cause be recognized and removed. It will be of little avail to adopt the official attitude, which would concern itself only with a surface healing, the concealing of the sore beneath being considered of more importance than to probe and excise it.

The average Englishman of today looks on a policeman as a sheep looks on a dog. It may be true that, should a wolf appear, he would risk his life, if need were, in the flock's defence. But wolves do not appear to be very numerous, and, meanwhile, the dog herds him here and there with little ceremony, or regard for his own wishes, and he is more conscious of these persistent irritations than grateful that he is being guarded from the sneak-thief or the confidence-trickster, till he be sufficiently fattened for the tax gatherer's knife.

It may be reasonable that a burglar should live in fear of the police, or that a householder should live in fear of burglars, but there are thousands of honest men, and tens of thousands of women, who, if they should hear a detective at the front door, and a burglar at the back, would be more relieved by the departure of the former visitor. To fear either the police or the criminal population may be inevitable, but to go in fear of both at once seems a hard fate for those who have to work for the support of these sections of the community.

The *Saturday Review*, in a recent article, touched one of the causes of this condition. It said:

THE POLICE AND THE PUBLIC, BY S. FOWLER WRIGHT

Much of the coldness between police and people that has been so noticeable of late is due not to the methods of investigating crime but to multiplication of the occasions of collision between the police and decent honest citizens. So minute and multifarious are the regulations about how we shall eat, drink, move and have our being that it is rare, these days, to find a respectable suburban paterfamilias who does not land himself in a police court twice a year, and, quite seriously, these irritations do subtract from the natural sympathy that should subsist between respectability and men in blue.

That is true enough, but there is no suggestion of remedy. The radical cure would obviously lie in a wholesale repeal of the complicated and costly burden of legislation which ever increases its oppressions, and this is a remedy which would be very generally welcomed. I suppose that if a political party were organized with pledges that it would not promote further legislation under any circumstances, but that it would devote its whole energies to the repeal of existing nuisances it would, *if it were believed*, be elected by an unprecedented majority. But that would require a boldness of imagination that is unusual among politicians, and we must expect that existing laws will not only be continued, but will be augmented incessantly.

It is one of the weaknesses of our constitutional system that members of parliament approach their duties with the assumption that the nation requires new laws as rapidly as they can wrangle them into existence, and that this stream of restrictions and penalties must never cease nor slacken. In the end, if it be sufficiently continued, it must cause a revulsion towards traditional liberties, through which the whole structure of bureaucratic tyranny may collapse, but, for the moment, we are concerned only with one of its subordinately vexatious consequences.

If it be allowed that we must exist as best we may under a weight of legislation beyond the possibility of our obedience or knowledge, there remains the question of by whom and in what spirit it shall be enforced. The *Saturday Review* points to an existing friction between the public and the police, which it attributes to this cause. It does not suggest the existence of any similar feeling against the judges or magistrates who administer the law, nor would it have been correct to do so. No such feeling exists.

The significance of this difference raises the question of what are the proper functions of the police, and what are, or should be, their limitations. According to the *Saturday Review*, in the same article, they have 'courts' of their own. Sir Archibald Bodkin, not a precision in the use of words, but writing in a mood in which feeling forms the phrase, in a letter to which later reference must be made, uses the same expression. Only he employs capitals—'the Police Court'. An emphatic man.

In both cases it is obvious from the context that magistrates' courts are intended—the high courts are not yet equally dominated by police influence, though the tendency is in the same direction—and this corruption of title has been steadily superseding, for many years past, that which is older and more accurate.

THE POLICE AND THE PUBLIC, BY S. FOWLER WRIGHT

Is it not a tacit recognition that the authority of the magistrates is fading, and that their courts are passing into a police control, which is leaving them with little more discretion than the grading of the penalties that the police require them to impose on those who are brought before them by the more virile authority?

Perhaps a consideration of this point may provide a convenient approach to our proposed enquiry.

CHAPTER II.

POLICE AND MAGISTRATE

What are the true functions of magistrates, and what are the powers and privileges of the courts over which they still nominally preside?

Let us avoid cant phrases, such as 'the administration of justice',[1] and endeavour to state these prerogatives accurately:

---

[1] 'The Administration of Justice' sounds a worthy occupation which should not be hindered, but it is an inaccurate description of the work of a modern law court.

Should I have a dispute with a neighbour over a boundary fence, and submit it to a judge for decision, he will presumably administer justice, or, at least, attempt to do so. Should he inflict a penalty upon a man who lights his fire with the wood of a public fence, he may still be so occupied, but if he fine a man for working an hour longer than the legal maximum or for building his own house without asking permission of a local council, he is doing nothing greater or nobler than acting as an instrument by which an organized section of the community coerces its neighbours to its own practices, and no question of justice arises, though that of injustice may.

THE POLICE AND THE PUBLIC, BY S. FOWLER WRIGHT

(1) They have authority to issue summonses requiring the attendance of persons against whom complaints are made of sufficient gravity, and not appearing *prima facie* to be of frivolous or malicious origin.

(2) For serious offences, or when there is reasonable cause to believe that a summons would be ignored or evaded, they may issue a warrant for the arrest of anyone against whom an affidavit has been sworn by his accuser.

(3) On the appearance of such persons before them, either by summons or warrant, they may deal with certain minor offences, without a jury, inflicting penalties of imprisonment, fine, or chastisement, and they may make enquiry into the more serious charges, either dismissing them, or, if there should appear to be a case to answer, committing them for trial to a higher court.

(4) In the event of such committals, they have the duty of fixing the amount of the bail which may be required from the accused or his friends, as assurance that he will attend his trial.

If a man under such a charge were to set up the defence that he had acted in ignorance of some arbitrary regulation, it would not be accepted, though it would be unanswerable, if justice only were the goal. He would be told, in effect, that he was facing a higher power than that of justice—the power of law. Let us therefore clear our minds of cant. English courts are not concerned with the administration of justice, but of law; if the two should agree, well, it is a very happy coincidence, but if they differ, justice will be elbowed to the wall without hesitation. If our law courts were to erect a statue to their own Deity, it would not be Justice, but Expediency, that would be unveiled. Expediency, with her own eyes lifted in reverence to the great god, COSTS.

(5) They have some other administrative functions, which do not concern us.

So far as the first two of these authorities are concerned, they have allowed themselves to be so entirely subordinated and directed by the police during recent years that they are frequently left without even the lip courtesy which is usually accorded to gentlemen who hold offices of nominal honour, from which the authority has departed.

The police will talk publicly of 'issuing' summonses in open contempt of those who still nominally exercise that discretion, and a chief constable has just given evidence at the enquiry which is now proceeding, in which he stated as a point in favour of the police, that they 'proceed' more frequently by summons, and less by warrant, than they did formerly, implying that even in the serious interference with private liberty which the issuing of a warrant involves, the magistrates are accustomed to take instructions from them.

The fourth of these functions, the granting of bail and fixing of its amount, raises more serious issues as it exhibits the magistrates as not only deferring their authority to the police, but gravely exceeding that authority, and trespassing upon the legal rights of accused persons, when they, are required by the police, as they are very frequently, to do so.

English criminal law is based upon the assumption that a man cannot be treated as Guilty of an offence which he denies having committed unless or until he has been tried and condemned by a jury of his fellow citizens, and, in the meantime, no one, either magistrate or judge, has any right to punish him for it, by imprisonment or otherwise.

It is to secure that protection that a serious charge must be brought before a magistrate without delay, and that it is one of his immediate duties, without any reference to the wishes of the police, or to his own caprice, to fix the amount of bail, though his opinion of the guilt or innocence of the accused, and of the gravity of his offence, may properly influence him in the amount at which such bail should be required.

Properly administered, this practice may inflict occasional hardship upon the friendless or the unfortunate, but it does secure that no man whose friends have confidence in his integrity, or in his courage to face his accusers, can be imprisoned in advance of trial.

But this constitutional right is refused almost daily by magistrates, taking their instructions from the police in open court, and sometimes even asking for such instructions when an application for bail is before them.

Such accused persons are probably not aware, or are not properly advised, that they have a legal right to apply to a judge in chambers, by whom bail would certainly be granted, unless there were a proper legal reason for its refusal.

It may be asked, why should the police concern themselves with such a question?

Should a magistrate grant bail on inadequate security, or in unsuitable cases, so that it would frequently follow that the accused would be absent on the day of trial, the discredit would fall upon him, and it would occur to no one to blame them.

But the answer is that there is no real doubt of this kind at issue.

In many cases, they have arrested a man against whom they have not yet worked up a case, and they know that they can continue their enquiries more freely if the magistrates will refuse bail complaisantly to their demand, so that a man may be subjected to an absolutely illegal term of preliminary imprisonment, not owing to the strength, but actually to the weakness of the case against him.

Other cases are of an even more flagrant illegality. It has become quite a frequent conclusion to a report of 'police' court proceedings to read, 'The police opposed bail, stating that other charges might be brought forward at the next hearing.' So that a man may now be imprisoned, not only on charges which have not been proved, but even for such as he has not heard, and which may never be formulated against him.

The arrogation of authority by the police being recognized as a fact, it remains to enquire whether there is any resulting disadvantage. The alteration which has occurred in this practice of granting or with-holding bail may supply the answer.

The magistrate is, or should be, primarily concerned for the rights and liberties of the community, including those of the accused person; the police are more immediately concerned with the preparation of the case which they are making against him. Their attitude is official, rather than social.

Human liberty has been so greatly curtailed in our country during the last fifty years that the mere fact that it has become a common practice to subject accused persons to a preliminary term of imprisonment before trial is not surprising. The significance of the fact lies in its being done without any legal pretext, and by an assertion of police authority for which there is no constitutional basis whatever. It shows also the direction in which the influence of this authority would be felt, if its extension were tolerated. If a man may be imprisoned, without the option of bail, so that the police may be facilitated in working up a case against him, it would be a short step to 'further the ends of justice' by the detention of important witnesses, who might not otherwise be punctual in their attendance at the projected trial. In particular, it would often be convenient for the husband or wife of an accused person to be imprisoned while their house is searched, or so that their correspondence could be examined.

The claim of the police to exercise a controlling discretion (or, perhaps, discrimination would be a better word), in the issuing of warrants or summonses, is extended from individual cases to whole classifications of illegality.

The magistrate, when a case is heard, will sometimes convict reluctantly, stating that the law constrains him. But where he is a blind tool of the law, the policeman claims to be superior to it. He will decide whether it shall be enforced in his own district, or may be disregarded. It is for him to decide whether its penalties shall be exacted, and for the magistrate to operate his decisions.

This attitude is illustrated very opportunely as I write by the announcement that motorists are to be warned instead of prosecuted for a first infringement of regulations in the London metropolitan area. The decision, in itself, is good—a short step in a direction in which many more should be taken. But a self-respecting magistracy—one free from the slavish impression that the nation is made for the law, rather than the law for the nation—would have taught the police this lesson at a much earlier date, refusing to have the time of their courts wasted, and their dignity reduced, by these endless trivialities. Instead of that, they have allowed their courts to be degraded by the imposition of endless vexatious fines for incidents which, if they required to be noticed at all, should have been the occasion of a call from a police inspector with a courteous word of explanation or protest, until the police themselves are alarmed at the public indignation which their petty tyrannies have awakened.

The obtuseness of the police mentality is shown very clearly in their initiation of bigamy prosecutions. It is true that the brutal stupidity of some of these proceedings is mitigated by the action of magistrates who grant nominal bail, and judges who pass nominal sentences. But the fact remains that, in many instances, there is no action involved, either immoral or antisocial, to justify any prosecution whatever.

Bigamy is a crime. It may be far worse than some of the homicidal acts which the law loosely classifies as 'murder.' To cheat a woman of her maidenhood, perhaps to occasion pregnancy, under the false pretence that she has the protection of a legal marriage, is among the basest of human iniquities. When it is done without impulse of affection, and with the object of robbery, it might well be argued that hanging would be too light a consequence. But deception is the essential factor of this criminality.

THE POLICE AND THE PUBLIC, BY S. FOWLER WRIGHT

When both parties are aware of an existing marriage, or of the doubtful fate of a long-separated Partner, the 'crime' may be nothing more than a technical legal irregularity, certainly less serious, by any sane standard of judgement, than are many offences of cruelty, or craft, or violence, which are punished by the infliction of a moderate fine.

In such cases, the dock would be better filled by those who give the malicious information on which the prosecutions are too often founded, or with the policemen who take the charges.

Yet when do we hear a word of rebuke or protest from magistrate or judge, when such cases are brought before them? The police have 'put the law in motion', and the legal gentlemen concerned must obey the crack of the driver's whip.

It cannot be asserted against this view that the police have no freedom of choice in the matter—that, like magistrate and judge, they must enforce the existing law, and that it would, therefore, be unfair if a judge should rebuke them sharply for initiating a needless cruelty. It is not necessary to consider the moral validity of such a premise, because we observe that the police do not recognize any such obligation. They claim for themselves, and exercise continually, a freedom of decision whether a breach of law shall be penalized or condoned.

Let us take two further illustrations of this new form of government by police bureaucracy.

There is a law against certain forms of gambling. It is a bad law, silly, inconsistent, and insincere. Under one of its absurdities, it has been held to be an offence to give a prize at a whist drive. The general sense of the community is not outraged by the giving of such prizes. It is the kind of law which can only continue to operate in a democratic state, where there is no evidently responsible individual who can be kicked in consequence.

It is a law which is broken continually in most parts of the country, but not in all.

There are places where such a reward cannot be given without prosecution and conviction following.

Who controls this difference? A locally elected authority? A bench of magistrates? Not at all. The magistrates simply do what the chief constable tells them. The decision is taken by the police. If the chief constable decides that the law is to be enforced, enforced it is. If he decide that it is to be ignored, no one will question his supremacy.

The second illustration is of a different kind. Suppose that a clerk were sent to his principals' bank to cash a cheque for the weekly wages, and, on returning through the street, he should drop the satchel containing the money, and I should observe the incident, and follow, and retrieve it. Suppose that I were to open the satchel, count the money, find that it amounted to £200, and then hand over £180 to the clerk, with the explanation that I retained ten percent as my commission on the transaction. Would he not, very rightly, claim the whole amount of the money for which he would be responsible, and appeal for help to the nearest policeman to recover it, if I should refuse to restore it to him?

Yet that is precisely the practice which is now followed by the police at the lost property office at Scotland Yard. All articles which are accidentally left in public vehicles, or which otherwise come into their possession, are valued, and they refuse to return them to their owners unless a sum equal to ten percent of that value be handed over to reward the finder.

We are too prone to regard the moral aspect of an action differently if it be done with formality; but apart from any such question, the legality of these detentions is extremely doubtful, and the result would be interesting, should someone sue the police for his property, instead of submitting to the imposition.

It is mere justice that the finder of a lost article should be compensated for any expenditure, or loss of time, which he may incur in preserving or restoring it; but such compensation can have no mathematical relation to the value of the recovered property.

It is a seemly generosity that will reward the finder rather in accordance with the value than the cost of the service rendered, but it is no part of the duties of the police to enforce generosity, which should be spontaneous.

If a man may properly retain ten percent of the property of another which comes accidentally into his possession, it is difficult to see why he may not retain twenty-five percent if he should consider it a more appropriate division. Or why should they not share equally?

Is it impossible for the official mind to comprehend that the moral quality of an action is not changed by legal enactment, or bureaucratic regulation?

This may be a symptom only—an unimportant symptom—of the evil from which we suffer, but a trivial symptom may be the evidence of a disease which is serious.

THE POLICE AND THE PUBLIC, BY S. FOWLER WRIGHT

The assumption of authority to intervene between the loser and finder of an article which may have been dropped or left behind, and impose a condition upon its restoration, whether it may have originated in the mind of a policeman, or of an official of the L.C.C., is an indication of the spirit of bureaucracy which encroaches further every year upon the freedom of the individual, and which is the radical cause of the friction between the public and the police, as it is of many other irritations, which are less important in themselves than as symptoms of the disease which they indicate.

A magistrate who is free from what may be called, in the jargon of the moment, the 'inferiority complex', and from that curious bureaucratic inoculation that 'the police must be supported', as though their organization exists rather for the coercion than the convenience of their fellow-citizens, might approach the investigation of a defended issue with these considerations before him—

1. It is improbable that the police will manufacture a baseless charge, and it is natural for the accused to dispute it.

2. Having brought a charge, the police naturally aim to substantiate it, and they are familiar with the nature and quality of the evidence which will be required for that purpose. Just as it is natural for a defendant to strain the facts in his own favour, so is it natural for the police to strain them into that which they know the court will require.

Beyond that, they are engaged in a duel in which they have the advantage of proficiency. It is the expert against the amateur. It is the duty of a magistrate to 'support the police' if he see them to be in the right, but it is equally so that he should be alert and jealous for the rights of the public, whom he represents, *and who are also represented by the man or woman in the dock.*

3. He should never forget that the onus of proof is upon the prosecution, not upon the defence, a principle of English law which is being increasingly disregarded in our criminal courts.

4. The question of whether the public interest really require that the case should be brought forward at all should always be present in his mind, so that the police should be suitably admonished in cases where official zeal has caused them to misunderstand the purpose for which they exist.

If the magistrates' courts were conducted in the spirit indicated, people would cease to think of them as 'police courts', and the present unpopularity of the police would very quickly diminish.

CHAPTER III.

POLICE EVIDENCE

In a recent prosecution otherwise unimportant, at the Quarter Sessions at Folkestone, the defending barrister is reported to have made this statement—

> In London nowadays people do not accept one police officer's statement alone since these big scandals. They always want more than one officer's evidence to support the charge.
>
> The police have got in such a state now that no one in London believes what they say.

In summing up, Mr. Roland Oliver, the Recorder, defended the police in these words—

> I have heard with regret that counsel should say that no one nowadays in London believes anything that a police officer says.

THE POLICE AND THE PUBLIC, BY S. FOWLER WRIGHT

> I am sure the jury, as sensible persons, will agree that his statement is very far from the truth. It is time such a thing was said on behalf of the police in this court, if nowhere else.
>
> In spite of what Mr. McDonald says, the police are just as good as other people, and, in addition, when you have a police officer in the witness-box, you start by knowing that he is a man of good character, which you don't always know about other witnesses.
>
> In all the scores of thousands of police officers in the country it is inevitable that amongst them there are a few unworthy of their office, but it is a monstrous thing to say that no one in London nowadays believes what a police officer says.

Similar allegations have been reported recently from defending counsel both in London and provincial courts, and have always provoked similar protests from the presiding magistrate.

Although we may allow a passing smile to Mr Oliver's logic, for how can we 'know' that a police officer is 'a man of good character' if it be 'inevitable that amongst them there are a few unworthy'? Yet all fair-minded men will agree with the spirit in which it is made.

The police are recruited from reputable citizens, of at least average intelligence. Except so far as it can be shown (if at all) that their training or experience as police officers is reasonably likely to result in moral degeneration, they are entitled to the presumption of probity.

But while assenting to the spirit of the Recorder's protest, and sympathizing with any member of the force whose veracity may be unfairly challenged, it is necessary to observe the nature (apart from the random wording) of the objection which caused it. This objection was to *the conviction of an accused person on the unsupported word of a single constable.*

Against this, as a general practice, it should have been unnecessary for counsel to plead. *He should have been able to rely upon the court not to convict under such circumstances, unless there were circumstantial corroboration, or a plea of guilty had been put in.*

It is a rule as old as civilization that not less than two credible witnesses shall be required to prove a disputed charge, and though there may be occasions and circumstances in which an intelligent magistrate may safely put this rule aside, he cannot safely make it a rule to do so. There are too many magistrates' courts where the evidence of a policeman is considered to outweigh that of any two of his fellow-citizens.

Even worse than the acceptance of the unsupported evidence of one man *because* he is a policeman, is the respect which is paid to what may be described as single evidence duplicated or multiplied through the mouths of two or more members of the force.

If two men observe an incident, they will not naturally describe it in exactly the same words. They will not have seen it exactly alike. Indeed, if one man repeat his experience, with a single-minded desire for accuracy, there will be differences in the two accounts, as his memory vanes.

If one man says, 'I was observing carefully, and I estimate the speed of the car at thirty-three miles an hour,' he may be attempting truth very honestly. If six men repeat the same statement, it is a concocted lie. Five of them are surely liars, and the other is less entitled to credit in view of the support he has enlisted.

Several of the police witnesses in the Enquiry now proceeding have emphasized that policemen are taught the laws of evidence. No doubt, these lessons save much time and trouble in the presentation of cases, but it is a knowledge which obviously places them at a great advantage in contrast to those against whom their charges are brought. The professional is likely to be more than a match for the amateur witness.

On this point I quote the evidence of the Recorder of Banbury before the Royal Commission at some length, because it has several points of interest. The report is taken from the *Morning Post* of Nov. 21, 1928.

In his answer to the Commission's questionnaire, Turrell said that when a statement was being taken, persons present were generally all police officers, adding:

Mr. Turrell—Generally speaking, corroboration by one police officer the statement of another adds little or nothing. Almost as a matter of course one police officer supports another.

The Chairman—You express rather unflattering opinions about the police.

The Police and the Public, by S. Fowler Wright

Mr. Turrell—There are very few cases in which the police bring charges which they do not honestly believe, but once they have embarked on a case there is a very strong feeling on the part of the police to justify their case. But I think it would be very dangerous to have a rule suggesting police evidence required corroboration. They must deal with it on the basis that they are perfectly fair persons.

The Chairman—I find it a little difficult to understand your attitude to the police, because a little later you say 'In some cases, particularly night charges and street offences the police take no pains to represent the true facts, but a stereotyped story which has no relation to fact. The evidence of one police officer supporting another, in opinion, adds little or nothing to its weight.'

Mr. Turrell—I think if one goes into a police court and hears the night charges nearly all the statements are exactly the same. I very much doubt, and have always doubted, whether the incidents happened exactly as the police described them. They tend to fall into a stereotyped form.

The Chairman—A stereotyped form. That may be, but you say, 'which has no relation to fact.' Is not that a grave charge to make against a body of men, to suggest that they are not generally-speaking honest and straight forward?

Mr. Turrell—I think when they have a man in custody and they are giving their evidence with regard to the incidents, they do not trouble very much about accuracy of details. With regard to the general charge as to whether the offence is committed I believe they are generally right.

THE POLICE AND THE PUBLIC, BY S. FOWLER WRIGHT

Mr. Turrell added that he did not want to put the matter in any unfair way to the police.

Mr. Lees-Smith, in his report on the Savidge Enquiry, alluding to this sinister quality in police evidence, used a phrase to which later allusion must be made, he called it 'mechanical precision'.

As I read that report, the phrase brought back a personal experience of many years ago when I had occasion to observe that 'mechanical precision' in *excelsis.*

I was on the jury at an inquest in Birmingham on a youth who had been picked up dead after a baton charge of police had passed over him. He was killed in Colmore Row, at the top of Livery Street. It was when Mr. David Lloyd George had been speaking in the Town Hall upon the Boer War, and some mild rioting had followed. I remember the police surgeon who amused the jury by enlarging on the almost criminal thinness of the skull of the dead youth, and by suggesting that, as he fell on his face, he might have knocked the back of his head on the curb stone, and killed himself, without the police having any responsibility.

I remember many things about that inquest, but most vividly do I remember the 'mechanical precision' of the police evidence;—the exactness with which every memory corresponded: the abruptness with which they stopped at the same point. The (then) Chief Constable of Birmingham had been in control in Victoria Square when the (quite unnecessary) charge had been ordered, but he had not ordered it. He did not know who had. No one knew. Had it started with out orders? Surely not. Every constable concerned, had heard the order given. There had been a voice from the void.

Had any constable struck a blow with a brandished staff? Not one. Or seen one struck? Not one. Or seen the fall of the running boy? Not one.

There was a constable named who had been on point duty at the top of Livery Street. The boy had been killed almost opposite where he stood. He gave his brief and negative replies to his friendly counsel freely enough, and then the veil fell. With a wooden stolidity he rebuffed every effort to extract the slightest suggestion of any further fact. He had seen nothing. He had heard nothing. He had thought nothing. Cross-examination ceased at last, baffled by the steady barrier of negative monosyllables with which he met it. I suppose that no one in the court believed him, but his evidence stood like a rock.

'Mechanical precision'—I think if Mr. Lees-Smith had given us that phrase twenty-five years earlier, the jury would have incorporated it unanimously in the inconclusive verdict in which (after repeated adjournments) those abortive proceedings terminated....

The constables stood by their superior officers, and one by one they swore stolidly that they did not know who had given the order to charge. Their chiefs stood by them, and did not require the name of the man who had struck the blow.

Against the enquiry of the coroner's court they presented the defence of a solid wall of perjury, obviously prepared and rehearsed with a knowledge of the laws of evidence, and it was legally impregnable, though there was

The Police and the Public, by S. Fowler Wright

probably no single person in the (then) half-million inhabitants of Birmingham who believed them.

CHAPTER IV.

CORRUPTION

So long as the police have their present powers, conferred or usurped, and so long as they are allowed to exercise them as they now do, so long must corruption continue. It is a plain fact, and it is best to face it. It may be repressed in Liverpool at one moment, or in London at another, but it will break out again. It is a natural consequence, and however evil it may be in itself—and I am certainly not disposed to defend it, it may actually mitigate other evils more serious and less tolerable.

I notice that one daily newspaper, when a comparatively trivial case of police bribery was proved in a London court, stated that the revelation had caused 'profound' public uneasiness. That is nonsense. The majority of the public would not be made uneasy, profoundly or otherwise, if they were convinced that every summonsable irregularity could be met by putting half-a-crown into the hand of the too-observant constable. Why should they? Is it to be supposed that people *like* the time-wasting annoyance, the publicity, and the higher tariffs of the magistrates' courts?

Their real trouble is that they don't know whether a bribe may be safely offered, or whether the constable may have the Pecksniffian meanness to report the attempt, with disastrous consequences.

I suppose that it is needless to say that I am not advocating the giving or accepting of bribes, I am merely recognizing a fact, which is a useful preliminary to the consideration of how best it can be endured or overcome.

It was recently stated (and denied) in the London press that bribery is habitual in connexion with the licensing of taxis.

I have no knowledge of this, one way or other, but if the system is similar to that which prevailed in Birmingham twenty years ago, it is a natural consequence.

At that time I was brought into close touch with the cab trade in Birmingham, being appointed receiver to a coachbuilders' business, which had been mainly occupied in the making and repairing of hansom cabs.

There were then many cab owners in Birmingham, a considerable proportion of them being the owners (or hirers) of single vehicles, on which the support of their homes depended.

Once a year, each man had to take his vehicle to the police-station for inspection. He received an order to have it repainted and repaired, as the Inspector might consider necessary. When this had been done, he had to take it again on the next 'inspection day' following, when it would be re-licensed, or refused for a further period, should the work not meet the Inspector's approval.

During these intervals, the cab owner was out of work, unless he could hire a temporary vehicle, and the Inspector favoured him with a temporary license for it.

In addition to this annual inspection, the Inspector, passing along the cab-rank, might stop before a vehicle at any time, and make an order for it to be repaired or decorated before it could be hired again.

This autocratic power was in the hands of two members of the police force, who were paid very small salaries, and against whose decision there was, in practice, no possibility of appeal. Is it difficult to realize the relations which would exist under such circumstances between them, and the hundreds of men with whom they were in continual contact, and over whom they exercised so arbitrary and vexatious an authority?

The Inspector stops, and looks at the (solid rubber) tyres, which are worn down somewhat near to the channels. The vehicle-license is ten months old. Shall he let them run on for the remainder of the year or shall he send the cab off the ranks today? It may be a life-and-death question to a cabman too deeply in debt to the coachbuilder to expect further credit, and who is relying upon the takings of the next few weeks to reduce the liability.

Further on the rank there is another cab, somewhat dingier than its companions. The Inspector looks at it reflectively. It is doomed, and its owner knows it. But the Inspector hesitates as he draws out his pocketbook, because he can write 'touch-up, and varnish,' which means, £2.10.0, and (with luck) that the cab will be back on the rank in five days, or 'repaint', which means £5, and a fortnight's absence.

May not Inspectors so placed, hesitating on the borderline of doubt, have been influenced by kindliness rather than corruption? Yes, often.

May not well-meant hints have been given, to be passed on from mouth to mouth, that if Inspector __ saw such a horse on the ranks again, a summons would be inevitable? Yes, many.

I am neither accusing individuals, nor the police generally, I am examining a system, and anyone with an average knowledge of human nature can judge its consequences for themselves.

It will be noticed that I am preferring old rather than recent illustrations, selecting, where possible, those that have come within my own experience, and avoiding personal references, excepting in the cases of Inspector Collins and the seriocomic figure of the Public Prosecutor; and, in these instances, to which I am coming, I should have left them in silence, had not the government, by its tacit or explicit support after their public exhibitions, given their methods a symbolic importance, which it is impossible to ignore.

But the mention of summonsing in relation to horses, brings me to the more serious power which the police exercised over the cab-proprietors at that period.

I am a lover of horses, and I know a little about them. I hate cruelty in any form.

The law which prohibited the working of unsound horses is good, and does good.

THE POLICE AND THE PUBLIC, BY S. FOWLER WRIGHT

But I love justice, as well as horses. The way in which the law was administered was grossly unjust, and this was known to all concerned *except* (we may hope) the magistrates who were ultimately responsible. *A summons always meant a conviction.* The police could always get a veterinary surgeon's certificate to support any allegation they made. Sometimes, a cabman, with a particularly strong sense of injustice, would bring a veterinary surgeon, or even two, to testify in his favour—there was no difficulty in getting such evidence by calling in witnesses *from outside the Birmingham area*—and in such cases the magistrates would 'support the police' by inflicting a heavier fine. It was a lesson to other cabmen to show greater docility, and not to occupy the time of the court with useless argument.

Now, so far as the legitimate object of these prosecutions was concerned, could it not have been obtained equally—indeed, much better—by the appointment of an expert surgeon who would go among the horses, giving advice and help to their owners, and only applying to a magistrate for a summons in rare instances—how rare they would be likely to be!—in which a cabman had refused to take his advice that a particular animal needed rest and treatment; and with the knowledge that, if he applied for a summons, the magistrate who investigated the case would (if possible) be one with some knowledge of horses, would *always* see the one in question, and would hear both sides impartially? It would have been a great advantage if, in such cases, the only expert witness allowed (if any) should be nominated by the magistrate, and should understand that the simple truth—and all the truth—whether favourable or not, was the real requirement of the court.[2]

Under such a system the horses would have fared better, whereas the summons issued (in practice) on the direction of the police-inspector, the brief routine evidence, prepared with an exact knowledge of what the court would require, the futile plea of 'not guilty,' expected, disregarded, and *expected to be disregarded* resulted in little beyond the obvious evil of the 'Five pounds and costs', which a cabman could not pay (if he would) merely by reducing his own beer, and which must therefore reduce his children's food, an his horses' corn.

Is it not obvious that, if it were desirable or necessary that public time or expenditure should be directed to the

---

[2] The *ex parte* expert witness is one of the major curses of the modern law court. Knowledge is so specialized that it is usually impossible for those who hear such evidence to judge its value, which is best assessed by the fact that another expert can always be hired to discredit it.

The expert may be quite honest, and he is always sure. (Sir Arthur Keith has just announced with 'scientific' certainty that fishes cannot learn by experience).

Mrs. Maybrick spent half her life in prison on the evidence of expert witnesses, which is now recognized to have been unsound. Probably the expert evidence on which several people have been hanged during more recent years will ultimately fall into the same category.

The evil would be mitigated if the expert could only be called at the order of the judge, and were nominated by him, but this would have other objections.

The employment of tame experts by the Crown, who *always give evidence for the prosecution*, is particularly vicious.

supervision of the vehicles and horses plying on the public streets, such extensive power should not have been left in the hands of two subordinate policemen, who, not in theory, but in fact, could obtain convictions in the 'police' courts with almost absolute certainty, whenever they wished to do so?

Is it not obvious that one member at least of the Watch Committee of the City Council should have been in direct touch with those concerned, ready of access, firm, sympathetic, conciliatory, and so controlling matters that the police would have felt that their reputations depended upon satisfactory results being obtained without the wasteful nuisance of continual prosecutions?

* * * * * * *

It may be said—it is easier of assertion than refutation—that English justice is systematically corrupt. It is not less so because the profits may not go to an individual pocket, but are openly added to various public funds, but it is difficult for most people to recognize a fact which is left in a universal silence.

A few months ago, a foreign woman in Liverpool made complaint to a policeman that a stranger had kissed her in the street. The man was arrested and, on the evidence of witnesses, was properly convicted. The magistrate fined him twenty shillings, the money was paid, and the next case was called. But the woman lingered, and being asked what more she wanted, replied, very naturally, 'that she was waiting for the money'.

THE POLICE AND THE PUBLIC, BY S. FOWLER WRIGHT

The daily press reported this incident with a general levity, stressing the foreign nationality of the woman, in explanation of the fact that she had expected any compensation for the admitted wrong she had suffered.

Yet had she brought the same complaint before an English tribunal of a thousand years ago, in the barbarous infancy of our race, there would have been two differences—the man would have been more heavily fined, the offence being more seriously regarded in the days of Alfred, and the money would have been handed to the woman, as its obvious owner.

Perhaps the difference arises from the fact that Saxon laws were (for the most part) made by the people for their own benefit, and that ours (for the most part) are designed by and for the benefit of controlling bureaucracies.

The illustration I have given is particularly simple, because the offence was entirely personal. The community was not outraged or injured in any way. Kissing in the streets is not illegal, though it may be so (for all I know) in a public park. The basis a complaint lay entirely in the attitude of mind of the kissed woman.

It would have been coldly reasonable had the magistrate handed the woman ten shillings, and said: 'We do not give justice here, either to citizen or stranger. It must be paid for. I assess the damage at ten shillings, fine the man twenty, and keep ten for ourselves.' Or he might have said, 'I assess the damage at twenty shillings, and cannot therefore order the man to pay more, but we're not going to give you justice for nothing, and I shall deduct fifty percent commission, which most business men regard as a liberal scale of remuneration,' but there is an effrontery of insolence in inviting the injured woman to the court, having her grievance proved, and then putting the whole proceeds of the fine into the coffers of the city which is responsible for the incident.

In considering this case, I am not deviating from the subject, I am cutting rather deeply into the core of the trouble.

For at the very root of these evils is the idea that 'the state' is something outside and above the individuals of which it consists. It is a perversion of the idea of ownership by a king or caste, and may develop an oppression more powerful and more sinister than any personal tyranny.

The most autocratic and lawless of rulers, had two people come before him with such a difference, would not have said, 'Very well, give me a sovereign', dropped it in his pocket, and imagined that his people would be satisfied that he had given an admirable example of the way in which justice should be administered.

If we allow the idea that the state or the law is separate from and superior to the individual, we shall find that, in practice, it will work out that the bureaucracy acquires that separation and superiority, and the law will become a scourge to the people who believe they make it.

* * * * * * *

There is another evil which must be utterly suppressed, if there is to be a spirit within the force which will discourage corrupt practices.

THE POLICE AND THE PUBLIC, BY S. FOWLER WRIGHT

Because it is difficult to obtain evidence against a night-club or a fortune-teller by decent methods, policemen are incited by their superiors to spy and cheat, or even to commit the offences which are to be the subject of the prosecution at which they are aiming, and it appears that men are found without difficulty within the force who are prepared to degrade themselves in these ways.

Is it reasonable to suppose that a man who is known by his fellow-officers to have been willing to spy and lie, or even to commit that basest of human actions, to win confidence that he may betray it—will have their respect or trust, or that of his superiors, or that; he can be relied upon to act with honour where his own selfish interests are at stake? Or that he himself will have any respect for his superiors who have prompted him to such courses? Or that the public being aware of such incidents, will have a high regard for the character of the force which cultivates them?

It is easy to defend these practices on the ground expediency. Thumbscrews could be defended in the same way.

But even on the lowest ground of expediency, the inevitable degeneration in mutual and self-respect that must follow, is a heavy price to pay for the convictions that are obtained by such baseness.

There has been agitation recently for the highest positions in the police-force to be filled by promotion from its own ranks. There is much to be said for this and it would be well if every new recruit could feel that the dignity of a Chief Constable was not beyond his ambition. But, if so, he must be expected to act in a spirit consistent with the goal at which he is aiming.

THE POLICE AND THE PUBLIC, BY S. FOWLER WRIGHT

Would it be tolerable for any man to hold such an office of whom it could be said truly, 'He used crawl under bushes in the dusk, to observe the actions of people who believed themselves to be in solitude, so that, if he should observe any intimacy between them which he considered a breach of propriety, he could put them to the pain and shame of arrest, after which he would publicly relate in detail what he had seen.'

Such a man is unfit to associate with decent people, and if we cannot classify him with the lowest of his kind, it is only because we have to remember the degradation of those who have incited his occupation. Beyond that, is it reasonable to suppose that people so accused or detected will not frequently offer bribes to avoid arrest? Or that men so employed will always refuse them? Or that men who accept such bribes will not be disposed to see such offences where others might not? Or be uninfluenced by the fact that they are expected to bring *some* cases in to the station? *Or that those who are indignantly conscious of innocence would not be the less likely to resort to bribery, and therefore in the greater peril?*

The matter should not require a detailed discussion. Its indecency—and done in the name of decency!—should be too evident.

But it is a procedure which could never have entered the mind of any responsible police-official, either to instigate or allow it, were he not already under the delusion that the intention of legislation is to provide occasions for the infliction of fines.

* * * * * * *

THE POLICE AND THE PUBLIC, BY S. FOWLER WRIGHT

The recent scandals which have been disclosed within the London area are of little intrinsic importance, and have no novelty to those whose knowledge and judgement had been sufficient to inform them of what is, and must be, under the prevailing system. Their interest lies in the official attitude with which they have been met. First by a blank denial, and then by the usual bureaucratic methods, concealing everything which it has been possible to conceal, evading everything which it has been possible to evade, and professing a zealous anxiety to deal with such incidents as could not be concealed or evaded. Then there has been the usual subterfuge—itself, at the best, a plea of incompetence—the appointment of a Commission of Enquiry. Also, there have been two or three prosecutions of police-constables for bribery or perjury, who have been punished with a severity graduated on what (it may have been supposed that) public feeling demanded, rather than the merits of the cases themselves, and a street-vendor of cheap jewellery, who offered a policeman five shillings not to arrest him, has been fined twenty-five pounds for that shocking depravity.

There has been the Adele case, in which two constables were convicted (probably correctly) of what may be one of the basest crimes that can be imagined, but which may be (comparatively) venial under easily conceivable circumstances. They were obstructed by the nature of their own defence. Having denied that certain incidents occurred at all, and being discredited in that denial, they were finally judged upon an account of those incidents given by their accusers, to which they could offer no alternative. But I suppose that no one as unprejudiced against the police as I certainly am (in spite of some things which are true, and must be written), could study that evidence without concluding that the whole history of those incidents has not been told. On more than one point there was an absence of logical sequence, an insufficiency of motive, an improbability of procedure, which made the case for the prosecution less than convincing. After studying the evidence very carefully, I am disposed to conclude that the men may have been rightly convicted, in the sense that they were not innocent, but I am less sure that such evidence should have been accepted as conclusive. It is true that the inhabitants of the London underworld are largely in the power of the police, and that they should be firmly protected from any abuse of that authority, but it is equally so that the police are peculiarly open to false charges being brought by conspiracy against them, and are equally entitled to the protection and support of their fellow-citizens in the discharge of the difficult duties which have been laid upon them. But it would have required a very high courage to dismiss the charge at the moment at which it was brought.

There has also been a case in which a constable, of previous good character, admitted taking a bribe from a street book-maker, his defence being that he had been tempted at a time when he had been suffering from an accidental loss of money. Here the penalty of imprisonment which was inflicted certainly did not err on the side of leniency.

The taking of bribes should be suppressed with any necessary severity, but this was about as innocent an example as can be imagined. The man from whom the bribe was received was acting illegally, but was; committing no serious offence. He handed over part of his profits to the constable, as he would otherwise have done to the magistrate, who would have black-mailed him, in the name of the State, in the same spirit and with a larger greed. I am not discussing the ethics of betting in the street, or elsewhere, or whether it is reasonable that a bet should be legal if it be sent by telephone, and illegal if it be delivered by hand. The State does not suppress street-betting. It farms it—as it farms the ulcer of prostitution.

In view of the absence of any evidence of habit in this case, which appears to have been casual, under the temptation of the accidental loss, and with the previous record of good conduct before the court, the incident might well have been met by 'binding over' the accused, who, it must not be forgotten, was already punished with great severity by the loss of his position, with all the pension and other rights attached thereto.

The sentence may have been expedient, but it was merciless.

Severities of this kind may reduce or even stamp out the giving and taking of bribes, *for the moment*, but the practice will revive, if there be no radical change in the conditions which produce the evil, as certainly as a new crop of weeds will grow on ground that is cleared, and then left un-planted.

If the conditions are to be altered from which corruptions arise, there must be a fundamentally different conception of the duties of the police, a nobler ideality among their higher officials, a different teaching and training for the new recruit, and a higher standard of social morality in the magisterial administration of the law.

CHAPTER V.

The 'Voluntary' Statement

The 'Voluntary' statement by accused persons, which has been so conspicuous a feature of criminal—especially of murder—trials during recent years is certainly dead, and it might be very briefly dismissed had the police frankly admitted the practice which they had cultivated; but, bad as that practice was, it may be doubted whether its exposure has discredited the whole force in the public mind one-tenth as much as the stubborn stupidity with which they have lied in denying it.

The evidence of Inspector Collins, who was not ashamed to profess himself a specialist in obtaining these documents, will be dealt with in a later chapter.

It would probably be a great injustice to the police to assume that the mentality of Sir William Horwood is to be accepted as typical, but he was the Metropolitan Commissioner, he could speak with exceptional knowledge, and his evidence before the Royal Commission, stubbornly evasive from first to last, cannot be entirely disregarded on this issue.

The Police and the Public, by S. Fowler Wright

Inch by inch, under the skilful examination of Lord Lee, he was forced to admissions the gravity of which he did not appear able to apprehend, or to refusals of reply, which had the effect of admissions, while exhibiting his mental attitude with even greater clarity.

It is not an unfair summary of the whole substance of his replies to say that he considered that the way in which statements were obtained from prisoners and others was useful in obtaining convictions, and that he was indifferent to any other consideration.

In almost every sentence he uses such phrases as 'the ends of justice'—'the interests of justice'—'the course of justice'—and he is not concerned with justice at all, in the nobler use of the word, but the implication is the obtaining of criminal convictions. That is the goal, to be reached by whatever means, and he is reluctant to admit even the possibility of trickery, duress, or any form of injustice (in the higher meaning of the word), occurring in that pursuit, and is obviously little troubled if it should do so.

Here is a typical abstract from his evidence. He has been protesting that the recent Home Office instruction in regard to questioning witnesses whose personal character is at stake 'is likely in many cases to defeat the ends of justice', and Lord Lee is questioning him on the position which he has taken—

We gather from your evidence that you are personally of the opinion that the administration described in the instructions is likely in many cases to defeat the ends of justice.

THE POLICE AND THE PUBLIC, BY S. FOWLER WRIGHT

Sir William—I do, because about three days after the Savidge Tribunal report I had a case as nearly as possible like the Savidge case. We overcame the objections of a witness to give evidence in the case.

The Chairman—You mean she did not object?

Sir William—She objected strongly, but we persuaded her in the interests of justice that she should speak, and she did. It is our duty to detect crime as well as to prevent it.

The Chairman—We are here to consider the liberty of the subject as well as the interests of justice.

Sir William—No police officer has any right to extract a statement from anybody.

The Chairman—We know it is the law, but do you think it is fully and generally understood by the public, and particularly by the poorer section of the public?

Sir William—I see no reason why it should not be. There is plenty of publicity given to the fact.

The Chairman—Do you think the ordinary man or woman realises fully that if the police ask them a question that they are at liberty to say 'No'?

Sir William—I really cannot answer that question.

The Chairman—Anyhow, the right is theirs.

Sir William—The policeman is not asking for his own amusement, but *in the interests of justice*.

Is it an unfair inference that Sir William Horwood cared very little whether or not people were unaware that the police have no right to force evidence or admissions from them?—Even, that it might be a good thing for 'the ends of justice' should they remain under that delusion?

The Police and the Public, by S. Fowler Wright

Pressed for an explicit reply, he becomes mulish. He 'cannot' answer that question.

English freedom, still a tradition, though little more, means nothing to him. If the citizen of today, cowed and bewildered by the innumerable laws and bylaws that control him, is ready to suppose that he must dance to any tune a policeman calls, under vague but no less terrible penalties should he refuse or delay to do so—well, what could be better? 'The ends of justice' will be served. Cannot Sir William understand that even the pleasure or advantage of convicting a criminal may be bought too dearly?

Faced by the suggestion that improper methods of obtaining statements from persons accused of serious crime are practised by the police, Sir William made this remarkable admission, 'The defending barrister makes the allegation. *I do not know of any murder case recently in which the allegation has not been made.*'

The examination continued from that point:

The Chairman—What steps do you take to ensure that there are no grounds for the allegation?

Sir William—The instructions in the instruction book and in the general police orders. Every officer is carefully taught when he joins the force, when he goes up for promotion, and when he passes into the C.I.D.

The Chairman—There is the allegation of cross-examining witnesses many hours at a stretch. In the Savidge case the number of hours Miss Savidge was examined were described as excessive from the point of view of physical endurance.

Sir William—I don't agree that she was cross-examined. She made a statement.

The Chairman said he wanted that point explored to the bottom in the interests of the police and in the interests of justice, and he wanted witnesses to help the Commission.

Sir William—I must be careful in answering a specific question. I cannot admit that any pressure in any shape or form was put on Miss Savidge.

Notice the evasive reply to the first question, to which a direct and honest answer would have been 'None'.

Notice the refusal to 'admit' that Miss Savidge was cross-examined. He does not say she was not. No sane man could, unless he wished to conceal his sanity. But he will not 'admit' it. He 'must be careful'. He obviously considers that he is there, not to help the Commission, but to defend the Metropolitan police, and he is a faithful partisan, though he cannot be described as a very intelligent one.

The only point which troubles him in connexion with the continual protests of different prisoners that they are tricked into signing statements which do not really represent what they intended to say, is that counsel cannot be prevented from mentioning these protests. 'I can see,' he says, 'no possibility of preventing such allegations being made from time to time.'

That is all that interests him. But if he can see no such possibility, other people can. There is the simple and satisfactory method of suppressing the practices from which these allegations arise.

Questioned by Mr. Brownlie, his replies are such as to need no comment.

—If anything of that character was to take place at a police station, would you know?
—Yes; I should know. *It would be reported to me.*
—If it did take place, and was not reported, how would you know?
—The only way I should imagine would be that I should get some definite specific complaint from someone which I could investigate.

Does Sir William ask us to believe that if his subordinates should obtain a statement by improper means, they, or one of them, would make a complaint to him, against themselves, and that he would then investigate it?

Or that the prisoner could obtain access to him without the knowledge or prevention of the officers concerned?

Or that he would believe the word of an accused person against that of the policemen? Would it not be most natural for a prisoner in such a position to make his complaint to his own legal advisers? And we have seen that Sir William will not listen, even to them. Such allegations are 'always' made, and therefore, Sir William asks us to believe, are 'always' baseless.

If Sir William Horwood can be accepted as representing any considerable proportion of the Metropolitan force, the task which Lord Byng has undertaken is not very enviable. But we need not readily believe it.

The Police and the Public, by S. Fowler Wright

Perhaps we have given too much space to Sir William. Let us consider what these 'voluntary' statements are, and how the police have been accustomed to obtain them.

In the course of the age-long growth of the constitutional liberties of the individual which are so rapidly disappearing, two safeguards were secured against the oppression of an accused person. One was that no man should be led either by torture or trickery to incriminate himself: the other was that no man could be imprisoned without being brought before a magistrate.

The Metropolitan police are impatient of both these safeguards, and have successfully overridden them.

The liberty of the subject does not further the 'ends of justice', and it must therefore go to the wall, legally or illegally.

It is often convenient to arrest a man against whom it is hoped that a charge can ultimately be made, but while there is not even the vague outline of a case on the strength or weakness of which a magistrate could be asked to grant an adjournment, and refuse bail. Therefore the man is 'invited' to the police station, and having been too foolish or too timid to refuse, he is not 'arrested' but 'detained'. Sometimes he is afterwards charged. Sometimes he is ultimately released 'through lack of evidence'.

In *either* event he has been subjected to an absolutely illegal term of imprisonment, for which he could bring an action against those responsible. But the legal fraternity has shown as little disposition to offer battle to the police on this issue as have the magistracy or the press, and so the abuse has grown, till it is carried on with a contempt of liberty and law such as we should have to go back some centuries to excel, or even to equal.

The other obstacle to their desired methods—the regulation that prisoners shall not be questioned without a caution—is evaded by the trickery of arresting a suspect on some other charge, which may itself be baseless. Then the arrested man is drawn into conversation upon the crime of which he is suspected, and concerning which there is no legal need to caution him, as there is no charge being made.

After that, we find him, by whatever transitional process, seated at a table, surrounded by police, one of whom is writing out a statement on foolscap sheets which he will finally sign, and after which he will be charged with the crime of which he has not been accused previously. It will then be found that the statement he has signed, though it may be an explicit denial of his guilt, or an account of his casual and innocent connexion with the event in question, will most curiously happen to contain innocent-seeming admissions which are exactly what is required to support a theory of his guilt on which the police have already been working.

Now, apart from consideration of the contemptuous evasion of law which this method requires, the most important question is, are these statements properly obtained, and do they represent a true and fair account of the incidents to which they relate?

Is 'justice' furthered, at least in the lower sense of the convictions obtained being those of the guilty?

Is it a system which, even if it could be shown that it is not necessarily unfair and has not been abused already, is incapable of being so abused, without any proper remedy being available?

I suppose that, even if there be difference over the earlier questions, there can be only one reply to the last, and that alone should be sufficient condemnation; but I suggest, not merely that such statements are not fair or accurate, but that fair and accurate evidence *cannot* be so obtained. The procedure is vicious in itself, quite apart from the methods or objects of those who use it.

Again I am able to draw an illustration from my own experience, which, though it was not concerned with any criminal procedure, offers a convincing analogy.

Many years ago I was asked to make a statement in connexion with some legal proceedings then pending.

The statement was taken by a court official probably of higher legal training in such matters than the average detective, presumably quite impartial, and having no possible interest in the subject with which the statement dealt.

I could have dictated the facts accurately and clearly to a stenographer in about ten minutes.

I remember that the writing out of the statement occupied about two hours—from three to five—and when it was passed over to me with a request to initial each sheet, I was impatient to be gone, and disinclined to consider its wording closely.

Glancing over it, I remember my impression that there was scarcely a single sentence in which my own words had been used. Scarcely one that had not lost in exactness through the interposition of another mind.

After a few minutes of silent consideration I realised that there were a few statements which were definitely false, and that I must either confine my alterations to those, or decline to sign it unless it were completely rewritten.

What was wrong in the main was an error of perspective, which could not be adjusted by verbal alterations. He had not written down what I said, but what he thought I meant, or inferences which he had drawn with not more than approximate accuracy.

I remember the alteration which I made in the first line, and I give it as an almost perfect illustration of the radical objection to this method of obtaining evidence.

In commencing the statement, he had asked my profession, and I had replied that I was an accountant. He had then asked, in a conversational tone, whether I were a member of the Society of Chartered Accountants, and I had given a negative reply.

At that time, the accountancy profession was divided into several rival societies (as it still is), and there were also many members of the profession who practiced independently. There was acute friction within the profession owing to the Chartered Society having promoted legislation (abandoned after repeated parliamentary defeats), to force the whole profession to join their body.

The official may have had little acquaintance with the actual position, but he must have had a vague and inaccurate idea that the Chartered Society had some preferential legal status. He had interpreted my reply into these words.

"I am an unqualified accountant."

When I altered it to 'fully qualified', he expressed surprise, and explained that he had not inserted the word with any derogatory intention, and I accepted that assurance.

But that is not the point, nor would it reach the point to discuss whether his description were accurate. The point is that I *had not stated it; should not have said it; and did not admit it to be a proper description.* Yet it was so written by an experienced officer of the court, who had no object to serve by inaccuracy.

How much less accurate is such a statement likely to be when written by one who has a pre-conception of the facts in his own mind, to which he is constantly aiming to bring the narrative to conform?

How much less accurate is it likely to be, when taken from one who may be less practised than I may have been in the use and control of words, whose vocabulary may be smaller, who may be less able to apprehend the finer shades of meaning and implication?

Even with the most honest intention, even with the utmost legality of occasion and method, it is a form of taking evidence which is essentially inequitable.

If such statements are to be admitted in evidence at all, if they are really 'voluntary', then it is mere justice that the accused should be as free to withdraw as he is to make them.

Certainly, there should be a rule that they are withdrawn, as a matter of course, on his assertion of inaccuracy. For he is the only man who can possibly tell whether they represent what he wished to say, and no one is in a position to contradict him.

Further than this, if a man who is able to write express a desire to make a statement, it is difficult to see why anyone should be with him at all. He should be provided with ink and paper, and a wastepaper basket (for his first effort, even were he a practised journalist, would be unlikely to be satisfactory), and left in quietness.

A voluntary statement *cannot* be obtained by question and answer, because it must follow the general direction of the questions asked, which must be that of the questioner's mind. This is probably one of the reasons that the taking of these statements occupies such lengthy periods. The prisoner wishes to say certain things which are *not* replies to the questions asked. The examiner wants answers to the questions he puts. The resulting progress is slow and digressive. It is an abuse of words to assert that a prisoner has not been cross-examined to obtain the resulting document, and the mere fact that it does not include the questions which produced it is sufficient to render it worthless.

Even the report of the evidence of a witness publicly and freely given, under the protection of a judge, and with his counsel watchful to interpose if necessary, and prepared to re-examine him on any point left doubtful, would not be regarded as satisfactory by an Appeal Court if it were given as a continuous paragraph, without the questions which had elicited it, or with those questions sufficiently woven into the narrative to make it intelligible, as though they also came from the mouth of the witness.

A voluntary statement is one which is the spontaneous expression of its author's mind. It must be written by him, or dictated freely, and without disconcerting interruption.

An examination by question and answer is a quite different process. It amounts to a preliminary trial of the accused, and it is an intolerable injustice that such trials should take place when he is confronted only by those who are preparing the case against him, without an impartial judge, without legal assistance, alone and friendless, and only able to offer his unsupported word as to what has occurred should there be subsequent difference concerning it.

But the taking of 'voluntary' statements by the police is not confined to those so obtained from probable criminals whom they have entrapped for that purpose. They are taken (and may be quite necessarily and properly taken) from witnesses and other interested or wronged parties to the issue with which they are dealing.

It was the taking of one of these statements which suddenly concentrated public attention upon the procedure practised by the police in the Metropolitan area, and which invites a detailed examination, not because it was, in itself, of special importance, or dealt with a specially important incident, but because there has been an elaborate enquiry to elicit the facts, and they have been largely disclosed, and have been the subject of two reports from the three Commissioners appointed to conduct the enquiry, of which one—the Majority Report—was adopted by the Government of the day, and publicly accepted, although the partiality of its comments, and the grossness of its omissions, represented a bureaucratic triumph more important and more sinister than were the incidents which it was appointed to investigate.

The Police and the Public, by S. Fowler Wright

CHAPTER VI.

The Savidge Enquiry

I have endeavoured, and I am still endeavouring, to avoid allusion to individuals so far as is possible. Had the Government taken the plain path of honesty when the two Savidge Reports were before them, they would have repudiated the Majority finding (which condemns itself, even to the most casual reader of the evidence which was brought before it), required the resignation of Sir Archibald Bodkin, and dealt promptly and suitably with the police officers concerned.

Had that course been taken, it would have been possible to avoid any direct allusion to these persons, or the incidents through which they became conspicuous.

Instead of that, the Government accepted the Majority Report, and defended it in public debate in the House of Commons.

Had the feeble and divided opposition in that House possessed a leader of first-rate fighting ability (in which case it might not have been so feeble or so divided), the Government must have fallen, as our parliamentary history shows that others, as strongly entrenched, have done from some slight-seeming, unexpected cause.

Against the tactical skill of Disraeli, the passionate eloquence of Gladstone, or the steel-cold logic of Joseph Chamberlain, no government could have held its front unbroken in defence of a document so clumsy in its evasions, so obvious in its prejudices, and so stubborn in refusal to 'admit' (as Sir William Horwood would say), any unpleasant fact, if the barest hope appeared to lie in the refuge of silence, or the audacity of denial.

* * * * * * *

We must now advance from the abstract consideration of the voluntary statement to the personal evidence of one who appears to have specialized at Scotland Yard in the obtaining of these documents; one who is (we are told), assisted by Nature with a kind and fatherly manner, by which he charms his victims while he destroys them; and one whose methods have been such that he has (he says), been congratulated by judicial authority nearly a hundred times.

The case concerning which he gave evidence was of no original importance, and, however satisfactory the result may have been to those whose characters were assailed, it is a real hardship that it should have had so much continuing publicity. But a brief summary is essential to an intelligent consideration of the events which followed.

One evening in the spring of last year, a middle-aged man and a young woman were seated on chairs in a quiet place in Hyde Park, when they were approached by two men in plain clothes, who said that they were police constables, and that they had observed them to be acting in a way offensive to public decency, which they denied. The constables arrested them both, and took them to a local police-station.

The next morning they appeared before a magistrate, and the constables repeated the charge on oath. The male defendant proved to be a well-known public man, Sir Leo Money, and after an adjournment of the case, and after hearing his evidence, the magistrate had no hesitation in dismissing it, without putting the female defendant to the ordeal of giving evidence, and he emphasized his opinion of the groundless nature of the charge by giving costs (£10.10.0) against the police, which magistrates are seldom inclined to do.

The case would have attracted less attention had it not borne some resemblance to others which had occurred previously, in which men whose public character was of consequence had been put to great expense and anxiety in successfully rebutting more or less similar accusations. It became known to the public that the Metropolitan police had a custom of sending out constables in plain clothes, to hunt in couples, in Hyde Park and elsewhere, for the express purpose of lurking where they might observe anything which would justify them in bringing such a charge, and that these men did, in fact, bring a steady stream of people to the police-station, scores in a month, who could only oppose their denials to the evidence of the constables, and who were, almost invariably, fined and released on the following morning. If they were persons of no public interest, the proceedings were not reported in the daily press, and they were unlikely to do anything to make their experience public, nor had they any reasonable prospect of securing redress, had they been improperly charged and convicted.

The result of these revelations was a measure of popular discussion as to the necessity or propriety of sending out plainclothes officers for such a purpose, the possibilities of its abuse, the openings which it gave for blackmail, and other considerations of police procedure not directly at issue, but on which there was an amount of public distrust which became articulate as it might not have done apart from this provocation.

The particular incident narrated was the subject of a question in the House of Commons, to which the Home Secretary very properly replied that he would have enquiry made as to whether there had been perjury, or some less offence, on the part of the constables concerned; and, to fulfil this promise, he gave instructions that the shorthand notes of the proceedings in the magistrate's court, and all other relevant documents, should be sent to the Public Prosecutor, with a request to him to investigate and report upon them.

The course taken by the Home Secretary does not appear open to any serious criticism. Even should it have been clear to his mind that the nature of the case did not admit of further evidence being procurable, nor of anything further being done for those whose characters were already vindicated, nor of any proof of perjury being possible, where there were two witnesses on either side, and the possibility of honest mistake could not be entirely eliminated, he might yet have felt that it would be well to refer the matter to the official specially appointed for such purposes, for his opinion and report upon it.

But the spirit in which this reference was received was suddenly revealed to an astounded public by an incident of a few days later, when a police motorcar drove up to the place of business where Miss Savidge (the young woman who had been charged with Sir Leo Money), was employed, and removed her without previous warning to herself, or the knowledge of her friends, to Scotland Yard. The car contained a police-matron, to assist if necessary in persuading her into the car—to 'comfort' her is the police word—but the need for this comfort or chaperonage ceased when she was on the police premises, and she remained for several hours in a room with two policemen only, at the end of which time she was allowed to go, having signed a statement which, while it did not expressly incriminate her in any serious particular, was so worded that it destroyed any possibility of prosecuting the two constables for perjury in relation to the events with which it dealt.

The following morning she signed another statement at the offices of Sir Leo Money's solicitors, in which she gave a detailed account of her experiences of the previous day, which, if it were true, showed the senior officer concerned to be, in several ways, unfit for the position he holds, and in which she alleged that the statement she had signed had not been worded by her, had been dictated by one of the officers (Inspector Collins) to the other, and did not convey a true impression either of the events themselves or of the answers she had given to the endless questions which had been rained upon her. She had signed it, *inter alia*, because she had been too tired for further argument, and because she had been assured that, if she did so, she would hear no more of the matter.

Before the police were aware that any investigation was proceeding into the way in which they had dealt with Miss Savidge, they had made an attempt of a somewhat different kind upon Sir Leo Money, which had been unsuccessful, and which had led to his solicitors receiving what we may hope to be the most extraordinary letter ever issued from the office of the Public Prosecutor, and when the matter was again mentioned in Parliament some further action became inevitable.

Whatever might have been Miss Savidge's experiences in Scotland Yard, the method by which she was taken there was beyond defence, as it was beyond denial, and the police excuse that they could not have forced her to go had she known and exercised her right of refusal, because their whole proceeding was a lawless bluff, did not improve their position in the public mind.

Faced with this position, the Government ordered a public Enquiry into the circumstances of her examination, and appointed three Commissioners to take evidence and report upon it.

Unfortunately, the matter had already come to be regarded by many as a political party question, which it obviously should not be, this arising from the fact that Sir Leo Money is a prominent member of the Socialist party, and that the Home Secretary has some executive responsibility for the Metropolitan police whose conduct was challenged.

THE POLICE AND THE PUBLIC, BY S. FOWLER WRIGHT

This being so, it was an error of judgement on the part of the Government to have appointed members of the Tribunal who might be expected to approach it with a party bias, and it was most unfortunate that when they reported their conclusions, they should have exposed this difference.

The Chairman of the Commission was a retired judge, of a very Conservative temperament. He prepared a Report, which was also signed by a second member, a Conservative member of parliament. The third member, Mr. Lees-Smith, a Socialist member of parliament, declined to do so, and after some delay and vain efforts to induce him to conform to their Majority findings, Mr. Lees-Smith issued a separate Report, which, in the most serious issues involved, directly differs from those of his colleagues.

On one point the Reports are agreed. The account given to the Tribunal by the two officers cannot be reconciled with that given by Miss Savidge, and the differences were not such as could arise from honest error. Either the two officers or Miss Savidge committed deliberate perjury before the Commissioners. The Majority report places this stigma upon Miss Savidge. Mr. Lees-Smith places it upon the two officers.

In due course, the Reports were debated in the House of Commons, when the Majority Report was adopted by the Government and received the assent of the House— after a debate which revealed the intellectual weakness of the Opposition, and by a vote which was given on merely party lines.

The Government, by adopting the Majority Report had committed themselves to the whitewashing of the Public

Prosecutor and the police officers, if not the police methods concerned, but though they had obtained the vote for which they had asked, they could not fail to realize that the moral victory was not theirs. The two Reports still existed, and they can bear only one interpretation to any careful and impartial reader, even though he may not have studied the more damning evidence of the Enquiry itself. They realized that the matter could not be permanently silenced by public announcements of the number of criminals in London, and similar irrelevancies.

They appointed another Commission to enquire into police powers and practices, calculating that it would take a year (if not two) to complete its labours, and hoping that they had shelved the matter successfully till after the date of the next election.

But the unavoidable flaw in this policy of evasion was that they had already been forced by circumstance to give one decision—that upon the Savidge Reports.

On this, the strength of their position is arithmetical. They said, 'We are obliged to accept the Majority Report—it was a case of two to one.' Just as the Majority Report says, 'We accept the evidence of the two constables, against that of Miss Savidge—it is two to one.'

To these arguments there is the reply that the Government itself made it two to one when it appointed two of its supporters and one opponent to the Savidge Commission, and the policemen themselves made it two to one, when they got Miss Savidge into their room to examine her without witnesses.

Against this numerical superiority there is an overwhelming logic of probability, and there are subordinate challenges in the facts that, in regard to the events precedent to her arrival at Scotland Yard, the evidence of Miss Savidge proved to be more reliable than that of the police, on points on which there were other witnesses, and that the evidence of Inspector Collins in regard to an attempt which he made to obtain another 'statement' the same evening from a Miss Egan was contradicted by that lady in important particulars, and when the evidence of her brother was offered to the Commissioners to support her version, they discreetly answered that they did not require it.

The question regarding the evidence at the Savidge Enquiry is not, therefore, was the element of perjury present, but rather, the perjury being present, by whom was it committed?

We have either to accept the Majority Report, which brands Miss Savidge as a prompt and very circumstantial liar, with an amazing faculty for realistic detail in her inventions, or to prefer that of Mr. Lees-Smith, with its inevitable implication that Inspector Collins led Miss Savidge, by the methods which she has narrated, to sign a statement which was not her voluntary composition, nor one which accurately recounted what she had intended to say, but which contained several carefully worded passages subtly designed to exculpate the two police-officers whose conduct he had been instructed to investigate.

We must believe that this statement was gradually written to his dictation by his assistant, during the course of hours of argument and questioning, his manner to her being sometimes persuasive and sometimes minatory, according to the degree in which she fell in with the suggestions he offered, or the measure of her protest against the wording in which he construed her answers as he dictated them, and that, from the advantage of his much greater age, and the authority of his official position, he treated her with a familiarity—not to use a stronger word—both of speech and action, which was an abuse of opportunity.

We must believe that, suddenly and unexpectedly finding the light of publicity turned upon the event, he conspired with his subordinate to deny utterly what-ever might be alleged to his discredit, and that, whether from desire to support the police, or the government or from honest prejudice or stupidity, he has had the endorsement of the Majority Report in the course he has taken.

The Majority Report does not merely exonerate him in general terms. It is explicit and detailed in its defence, and ruthless in its condemnation of the witness, who, through no fault of her own, was placed in such a position by the police themselves that she can have no one to support her own account of the interview.

If this defence is sometimes lacking even in a surface plausibility, it may be owing to the inherent weakness of the case, rather than to any inability of Sir John Eldon Bankes in the drafting of such documents.

His method is to enumerate, in his own words, what (he says), Miss Savidge has 'alleged' against the police, under six heads, and then to give his reasons for disbelieving her.

Before doing this, the Report endeavours to suggest that there is a preliminary presumption that the perjury which has undeniably taken place will have been on the side of Miss Savidge, because Inspector Collins has been 'commended by Judges upon ninety-three occasions for skill and ability in the performance of his duties,' and because she had had a night for reflection upon the first statement before she made the second.

We must return to these commendations of Inspector Collins, but, for the moment, it is sufficient to observe that, had matters gone as he must have anticipated, the Inspector might have had a ninety-fourth commendation from the Director of Public Prosecutions, for the ability with which he had obtained Miss Savidge's statement, and for the fact that it was so satisfactory a document, from the point of view to which the enquiry had been directed.

As to the night of reflection, most people will agree that it is quite as likely to arouse protest in the minds of those who have signed inaccurate statements, as in those who have signed accurate ones; and, as the Commissioners cannot have failed to realize, the conflict of evidence goes far beyond a difference as to what the statement contained. Miss Savidge made affirmation of incidents which the policemen totally deny, and which imply an extraordinary perversity of invention, if that denial be accepted.

There are some points in the affirmative evidence both of Miss Savidge and the Inspector which invite attention, but I will first take the Inspector's defence, as it is set out for him in the Majority Report.

I am first giving each of the numerated points which the Report sets out, then the conclusion which it appends, and then my own comments upon it.

(a) That the Chief Inspector terrorized her, and gave her to understand that she must tell the truth and that nothing more would be heard of the matter.

(a) Miss Savidge was not intimidated into answering questions. Chief Inspector Collins and Sergeant Clarke gained her confidence and at their request she answered questions freely.

Here the Report knocks down the ninepins which it has first erected. Miss Savidge had not alleged the Inspector terrorized her. This point is not very important, except as showing the spirit of bias in which the Report is written. Her evidence is fairly summarized by Mr. Lees-Smith in these words—

> Miss Savidge's evidence makes it clear that the officers were, on the whole, kind to her, although she complains that when they found it necessary, their attitude hardened and that they hustled her into statements which they, rather than she, wished to have made.

It was the obvious policy of the police to gain confidence, if they were to induce her to sign a statement to their own liking, and only to bring threatening pressure if, and as far as, more adroit methods might fail; and this is exactly the attitude indicated throughout by Miss Savidge's account of the matter.

Incidentally, we may observe that if the questions asked were answered as 'freely' as the police assert, and the Report repeats, and if, as the police also assert there was no cross-examination, the four or five hours occupied in taking the statement become incomprehensible. In this, as in some other points, the police have failed to observe that denial may go so far as to over-reach itself.

(b) That the Chief Inspector dismissed Miss Wyles from the room in order that he might conduct the interrogation without a woman's interference.

(b) Miss Wyles's presence during the interrogation was only dispensed with because Miss Savidge expressed herself as quite content that it should proceed without her.

Notice the 'only' and 'quite' which overstate the contention, and again show the prejudice which colours every conclusion offered.

Beyond that, it would be interesting to know in what part of her evidence Miss Savidge asserted that she knew the Inspector's motive for getting Miss Wyles out of the room. No one can do more than guess at the Inspector's motive. It is a thing which obviously ought not to have happened, in view of the examination which he had in mind, and of the nature of which Miss Savidge was ignorant. He suggested it, and must bear the responsibility. Whatever measure of consent Miss Savidge gave, she must have been asked to give it, and the volition was that of the one who asked her.

(c) & (d) That he made to her a most improper remark about not having had connection with a man. That in an improper and indelicate manner he carried out a demonstration of the way in which he suggested that she and Sir Leo Money were sitting in Hyde Park.

(c) & (d) The alleged demonstration did not take place nor was the alleged remark made. Miss Savidge was treated by Chief Inspector Collins and Sergeant Clark with no lack of propriety.

If this be the honest opinion of the two Commissioners who signed this Report, I suppose that they must be the only ones who have studied the evidence, and have reached such a conclusion—certainly so far as their first sentence is concerned. The second may be more disputable, as a matter of opinion, or of degree.

That Miss Savidge should have invented the remark in question, or the detailed incidents which she narrated without the most persistent cross-examination being able to disconcert her, is an improbability so extreme as to approach the incredible, and the blank wall of duplicated denial by which the two police-witnesses met it loses any weight which it might otherwise have when it is remembered that they also gave an account of the way in which the various details contained in the statement were spontaneously offered by Miss Savidge, which is an insult to any ordinary intelligence.

(e) That he inserted in the statement things she never said, and distorted what she did say to serve his own purpose.

(e) Miss Savidge's answers were not misconstrued or improperly recorded. She approved them at the time.

The Police and the Public, by S. Fowler Wright

Overlooking the grammatical eccentricity of this comment (most people approve of their own answers), we reflect that Miss Savidge had been under examination for at least four hours. At the end of that time she was asked to initial and sign fourteen sheets of foolscap, which she very foolishly did. The Commissioners think it is a fair deduction that 'she approved them at the time.' It is inherently improbable that she read them over carefully before she signed them, and the more we credit the police assertion as to the happy way in which the afternoon had been spent, the more unlikely it becomes.

Her own account is that she was so 'fed-up' that she was only anxious to get away, which is not at all difficult to believe. It does not logically follow that the police deliberately take long statements at one sitting so that they may be the more carelessly signed, but I have no doubt that it does, in fact, have that result, and it is scarcely possible that they are not aware of this consequence.

(f) That owing to the length of the interview she was so tired that she did not care what the police put down.

(f) No doubt Miss Savidge was tired, having been at work since eight o'clock that day, but she had had lunch and tea and was quite competent to understand what was said and done, as is shown by her detailed statement made to her solicitors next day.

This comment is worthy of Inspector Collins himself. No one had suggested that Miss Savidge was not 'competent to understand', and the expression is an evasion of the real issue. (As a fact, she could, at *any* time, only have had a partial competence, but the suggestion evades the true issue).

The suggestion that the fact that she was able to dictate a statement *the next morning* is evidence of her attitude toward her prolonged detention on the previous day, or of any physical condition resulting, might have a suitable place in the oratory of Sergeant Buzfuz, but perhaps that is not quite the same thing as saying that it is out of place in this Report.

Also, the Commissioners appear to have forgotten that they have already condemned her next morning effort as having been one of random imagination rather than accurate memory. Like the Inspector they have found that zeal may leave discretion in the breathless rear.

It is a relief to turn from special pleading of such a character to the Minority Report of Mr. Lees-Smith.

It is not only that it is written in better English and that it is more coherent and logical in its conclusions. It gives the impression of being an honest and intelligent effort to reach the truth without fear of favour either of persons or institutions. It is judicial in tone and temper. It does not avoid comment on such unpleasant facts as the correspondence of the Public Prosecutor, but it treats them with a careful moderation which, from that very quality, become deadly in its condemnation. It does not merely assert but gives argument and quotation, so that, even to any-one unfamiliar with the evidence given at the Enquiry or with the two Statements which were in question, it has a more convincing atmosphere.

THE POLICE AND THE PUBLIC, BY S. FOWLER WRIGHT

To anyone who has considered that evidence with a impartial desire for truth, the one Report has the effect of advocacy, and the other of judgement.

I have dealt with these aspects in some detail, because it is impossible to read the evidence of this Enquiry without indignation at the way in which a charge of almost incredible invention, supported by persistent perjury, is implied against Miss Savidge in the Majority Report, with the too-obvious purpose of 'supporting the police' against the major scandal which must have followed had it taken an opposite course, and because, though it was the general thought, everyone, in the face of that legal majority, has seemed afraid to write it.

There is another consequence of that attitude in that it became logically impossible to remove Inspector Collins from office, and while it is clear, from the subsequent evidence of Sir William Horwood, that the spirit in which he had acted was the official atmosphere of the Yard, it became possible to avoid the immediate issue by the appointment of another Royal Commission.

It is noticeable that the Majority Report was extremely careful to avoid any individual condemnation. Even regarding the method employed to get Miss Savidge to Scotland Yard, it is careful to say that the policemen concerned would be much to blame, but for the fact that they were acting according to their regular practices. Which, to the bureaucratic mind, is a sufficient answer to anything, and no one was, is, or ever will be, responsible for anything which happens in consequence.

For every personal word or action, where 'the system' could not be invoked for harmless condemnation, the two

Commissioners, after hearing Inspector Collins, gave him their unflinching support. They accepted every denial he made. They narrated his many previous judicial commendations. They explicitly approved the discretion which had selected him as the officer most suitable for such an investigation.

He becomes, therefore, symbolic of triumphant bureaucracy, and the evidence which he gave, and which has received such approval, acquires an importance which it would not otherwise have.

We will proceed to consider it.

CHAPTER VII.

THE SMILE OF INSPECTOR COLLINS

It is given to few men to foresee the consequence of their own actions.

Chief Inspector Collins, confident in his ninety-three judicial commendations, observing with satisfaction that Miss Savidge had been successfully decoyed into the 'nice room' at Scotland Yard, putting her at ease with his fatherly manner, suavely talking Miss Wyles through the door, and sitting down with his henchman to the inquisition which they had planned already, probably felt a degree of satisfaction which was only exceeded by that of a few hours later, as he surveyed the fourteen foolscap signed and initialled sheets, on which was recorded the evidence, so spontaneously volunteered, in which Miss Savidge, careless of her own reputation, had contrived, in spite of her ignorance of the legal issues involved, with a miraculous intuition, to say the very things—to use the exact words—which, without precisely accusing herself of anything of which she was admittedly innocent, would render it obviously impossible for two worthy members of the force to feel any further anxiety concerning an incident which was best forgotten.

How could he foresee that the young lady would be occupied a few hours later in making another statement, without his expert assistance to control its wording—or that anyone would have the temerity to put it forward against the one that she had signed already against the words of himself and his assistant, even against the weight of the ninety-three commendations and despite a Public Prosecutor spluttering with wrath in his office?

The answer is simple, and (for the Inspector) sad. He did *not* foresee it.

Yet we may observe that life is never without it compensations. If there were moments at a later day when he was to endure a cross-examination before which even his self-complacency was disposed to falter was he not to go on holiday at last with the congratulations of his companions in his ears, and in his pocket a report signed by a retired Judge of Appeal of the High Court, and an acquiescent colleague, which was suitably eloquent about his virtues, but became discreetly silent at the points at which silence was so eminently desirable?

Sir Archibald Bodkin also, a singularly modest man moved by honest indignation to the dictation of a minatory letter, how was he to know, as he worded the vague illegal threat of the concluding sentence, that all England would soon be reading it? An improper letter? Not at all. He had rather liked the sound of the final words as he signed it.

Anyway, it was a letter which had been issued by the Public Prosecutor of the realm of England, and if the Public Prosecutor wrote such letters, must they not be proper letters for Public Prosecutors to write?

But we must turn aside from the spectacle of Sir Archibald Bodkin, ejaculatory in the witness-box, almost inarticulate with wrath at the possibility that HIS conduct might have been criticized, and vaguely hinting at the dreadful language which he would feel justified in using under such provocation. We will return to him later.

The Chief Inspector will not swear. He is a very kindly man. He will smile, even when he thinks of the murderers (or, at least, those who have been convicted of murder), who may have regretted the 'voluntary statements' in which he specializes, or denied their accuracy. Did they have cause to regret them? Perhaps a laugh is the best answer.[3]

Anyway, they are dead now.

But we must not treat the Chief Inspector lightly.

We are about to observe him as a man of super-normal ability, of superhuman integrity. He is the man who never errs. He is the rock on which the police rely to roll back

---

[3] The *Times* report states that this dialogue took place between Sir Patrick Hastings and Chief Inspector Collins—

'You have said that you have been engaged in a number of murder cases. It is not unusual nowadays, is it, to find in murder cases that the accused has made a voluntary statement to the police?'—'Quite so.'

'Recently it is quite unusual for a murderer not to make a voluntary statement?'—'I cannot say.'

'It frequently happens that they regret it afterwards?'

The witness laughed as he replied: 'I don't know. I cannot express an opinion about that.'

the tide of calumny which has been rising against them. We will hear his record from his own lips. He ought to know.

This is what he modestly told the tribunal in response to the questions of his own counsel:

> He had been commended by Judges on ninety-three occasions for his skill and ability in the performance of his duties, and for his public services—he had been deputed to deal with murder cases in London and in the Provinces, had held instructional classes for the training of young officers in Scotland Yard, and had given lectures on methods of criminal investigation. *No complaint of any kind had ever been made against him by the public or by the police authorities.*

Ninety-three times! And the police had not complained, nor had 'the public'. Never once. We are not told what the prisoners may have thought—ninety-three, more or less, who, after all, were the most concerned. But we are told that the 'voluntary' statements of which we have heard so much in recent years—statements taken from men who were alone and unadvised, and many of whom could scarcely have followed the finer implications of the words in which they were put—statements made in the presence of groups of police officers who were the only witnesses as to how they were obtained, against the unsupported word of one suspected man—had *always* been accepted at their face-value by every judge before whom they had been produced. Never had a judge been found to criticize or reject a single one of these documents. Never once.

That, at least, is the evidence of Chief Inspector Collins. We may proceed to discover how far his word should be taken on any serious subject. If his allegation be true, there is this to be said.

It is held to be illegal to criticize an English judge during his tenure of office. If that be good law, it is very bad law also, and it is time that someone should have the courage to challenge it. But no man will ever make a deadlier attack upon a whole bench of judges than is contained in that assertion of the Inspector. *Never once* (he says), has such a statement failed to obtain commendation for those whose trickery had obtained it. Never once has its essential rottenness been put from the judicial bench in scathing words to the jury. Never once....

It is not wonderful, with such a record, that the Chief Inspector stands in the witness-box very confidently, though a girl has faced that ordeal for two previous days and has given detailed evidence which, if true, has shown him to be unfit not only for the position he holds, but for the society of any decent men, and one of the cleverest counsel at the English bar has struggled in vain to shake that evidence.

But the Inspector denies everything. He denies it in the confidence that his henchman will do the same. It will be two to one. Do they not know the law of evidence? And has it not been already shown in the few cautious words that have fallen from the Chairman's lips, that he is sound at heart? That he will 'support the police' No doubt some things will have to be modified for a time, but they will bend to the storm, and there are those who will see that it does not break them.

The public confidence in the police must not be shaken. The Chairman can be relied upon to give that thought due weight, and so can at least one of his colleagues. Against such an issue, who can weigh a girl's reputation seriously? Against that of a Chief Inspector and of a Sergeant of Police, what is a girl's word worth?

I am not going to waste many pages in labouring proof against the Inspector's veracity. The report of the evidence of Miss Savidge, and of his denials, exists for all who care to read them.

When I say that I am convinced that on all essential points she was a truthful witness, with all that that belief implies, I am not merely giving a lonely vote for the Minority Report, I am saying what is the belief of practically everyone who has given any serious study to the evidence of the witnesses concerned.

The Inspector's mistake was that, having commenced lying, *he did not know when to stop.* Confident in the knowledge that his henchman would support his statements, and that Miss Savidge could hope for no corroboration, he went on from credible or disputable lying to that which was incredible and indisputable.

He might have retained a measure of sympathy had he defended himself in this way—

'I admit that the account given by Miss Savidge is substantially accurate, but in all I did I was actuated by a real desire to reach the truth, and the methods I used were those in which I have been trained, and they have resulted in my being praised on ninety-three previous occasions. Can all the judges who have seen me present my cases, so simple, so conclusive, so complete, so that they could sum up without difficulty, and the jury could condemn without hesitation, have been altogether incurious, or unsuspicious, as to the methods by which such results were reached? Did they really think that there had been no foundations to lay? No scaffolding to be pulled down, and removed from sight when the finished edifice was presented to the admiring court? What *did* they think I had done to deserve such special commendation? Why did they always brush aside the prisoner's protests, or those of his counsel, if there were allegations against my methods, as there usually were?

'Why should I be told to go under the table now, when there have always been pats and tail-waggings when I have caught the rabbit before? (The wrong rabbit, maybe? Well, does it matter so much? You can't have a trial without *some* prisoner, can you? And I really did try to pick the right man.)'

That would have been an intelligible attitude, and he would have shown himself as no more culpable than, for instance, Sir Archibald Bodkin, or Sir William Horwood, both of whom have shown approval of the methods of which Inspector Collins is the finished product.

Whether he would have pleased his superior officers by such frankness, as he evidently did by the line which he preferred to take, must be doubtful. Anyway, he decided differently.

I have said that I will not waste many pages in a detailed consideration of the evidence in question. One or two illustrations must suffice, where a dozen of equal quality are available.

It is common ground that Miss Savidge was asked to describe what she was wearing on the day of the incident from which all the trouble had arisen, and it is a fact that the statement contains a very detailed description of it, including her underclothing, and that it includes points which would be useful to the defence of the two constables who molested her on that occasion, should the occasion for such defence arise.

Inspector Collins asks us to believe that he merely asked in a general way what she had been wearing that day, and that she immediately went into fluent detail about every article, inside and out, so that there was nothing for him to do but to remain silent while his assistant transcribed it.

Here is an abstract of her evidence before the Commission on that point—

> "Inspector Collins told me to stand up, and Sergeant Clarke also said, 'Yes, stand up'."
>
> "Why?"
>
> "To see the length of my skirt. They asked me questions about the length of my dress, and of my petticoat."
>
> "What did they want to know about your petticoat?"
>
> "Of what colour it was, and of its length."

or again, when she was being questioned by Mr. Lees-Smith—

> Mr. Lees-Smith—What did they say about the petticoat?
> They said: of course you were wearing a petticoat? I said yes, and they asked what colour? and I said Pink. They said, a very short one I suppose? I said, not extra short. They said: It must have been short if you were wearing a short skirt, and it was written down as a very short petticoat.

So her evidence went on, unhesitating and circumstantial, from point to point, and we are asked to believe that it was concocted of conversation that never took place, and incidents that never happened. And to believe this against the inherent improbability, amounting almost to the impossible, that she would have spontaneously given the kind of evidence of which the statement consists.

A question is asked, and an answer given which must have been expected. Miss Savidge states that the words 'as far as I know' were prefixed at the suggestion of the policemen, and after some argument with them. Inspector Collins says that they were her own expression. It would probably be understating the improbability to say that it is about a million to one against anyone spontaneously adding such a qualification to such a reply given under such circumstances, and its inclusion would make a vital difference to the possibility of prosecuting the two constables, as Inspector Collins must have known.

THE POLICE AND THE PUBLIC, BY S. FOWLER WRIGHT

When Miss Savidge narrates the way in which her answers were challenged and discussed until 'He got me tied up, until I wondered whether I really could remember,' we are asked to believe that it is the utter invention of one who had spoken so willingly and fluently to two policemen who were not trying to edit her evidence in any way, that, they had had nothing to do but to write down as quickly as possible the narrative with which she supplied them. And that it took (at least) four hours to take it down in this way.

The contention is an insult to any ordinary intelligence, and it is only because of the importance of the issue that I give space to a further example. I take this verbatim from Mr. Lees-Smith's Report:

(d) Miss Savidge states that in order to ascertain in what attitudes she and Sir Leo Money were sitting on the night of their arrest, Chief Inspector Collins placed his chair next to hers, first put his arm round her waist, then linked his arm in hers, and then took her hands in order to obtain some indication of the attitude in which they were sitting. While this was going on, he put to her various questions to ascertain their relative positions, and finally dictated a statement which entirely misrepresented the position in which she and Sir Leo Money were actually sitting in the Park.

Chief Inspector Collins asserted that the only question he put to her on this whole matter was:

'Miss Savidge, will you be good enough to tell me very carefully exactly how you were seated?' She then pushed her chair back from the table, thought very carefully indeed, crossed and uncrossed her legs, and carefully and deliberately said, 'We were very close to one another, and I was inclining towards him. I was sitting on his left; so far as I can recollect his right hand was clasped in my left, resting on my left leg, and my right hand was locked in his left hand. I cannot say whether my legs were crossed or not. This is as far as I remember.'

He put to her no questions after she began to make the above statement. It was not a summary of questions and answers, but a verbatim record of her actual words.

Is anyone prepared to discredit the account given by Miss Savidge as to the way in which this part of her evidence was obtained, in favour of the Inspector's assertion that she produced that involved sentence about the relative positions of five different limbs without any prompting question?

It is not only absurd in itself, but there is an inherent improbability in that *it is not Miss Savidge's manner of speech.* This may be a point which will appeal more forcibly to the literary than the legal mind, but it is, of itself, absolutely conclusive to anyone who is accustomed to such considerations. It is an additional proof, where no such addition was needed.

The Police and the Public, by S. Fowler Wright

It remains true that while there are many points, such as these, on which it is difficult to hesitate as to who should be credited, there are many others where it is simply a case of the word of Miss Savidge against that of the two policemen, and we must make our own choice as to where the truth may lie.

But there is this to be said, that wherever it is possible to examine the evidence on the issue of internal credibility, or where there is some supporting evidence available, as that of Mr. Saxe or Miss Egan, it is usually—indeed, as far as I have observed, invariably—Miss Savidge who comes best out of the test.

CHAPTER VIII.

The Public Butler

It is no part of my present purpose to discuss whether it be necessary or desirable that the organization of the administration of criminal law shall include a Director of Public Prosecutions. It may be observed that the country endured without this official for many centuries; and it may be an arguable proposition that a Director of Public Defences, to whom innocent persons might appeal for help when unjustly prosecuted, would seem to be a logical complement. But if we allow the necessity for this official, it may be generally agreed that it is an essential qualification that he shall be a man of cool and balanced judgement.

It might be added that he should be a man of sympathetic and tolerant disposition, one knowing that a prosecution of any kind is a social evil, which can only be justified by necessity.

The equal or greater need for a Public Defender was forcibly presented by a solicitor of over fifty years experience in the criminal courts, in a recent letter to the *Morning Post*, in the course of which he said—

> It has on several occasions been my duty, acting for clients of means, to prosecute criminals, and on these occasions I have been painfully impressed by the relative helplessness of the poor defendant. It is not possible for him, if he has a defence, to have it got up for him with anything approaching the thoroughness with which the case for the prosecution is got up.
>
> It is in the thorough getting up of cases, and not by the genius or eloquence of the Bar, that they are in the vast majority of instances lost and won; and when a prisoner in the dock is assigned a counsel and instructs him it is too late for any getting up to be done. Fortunately, most prisoners charged are guilty and the best the best counsel could do for them is to plead and to offer evidence in mitigation of sentence. But in the relatively few cases where the prisoner has a good defence, it is, in my opinion, desirable; in the interests of justice, that there should be some organization charged with and capable of the duty of first ascertaining whether there is a genuine defence, and secondly, of getting up that defence as effectively as the case for the prosecution is got up.

THE POLICE AND THE PUBLIC, BY S. FOWLER WRIGHT

Even if there be no public provision to ensure that an accused person cannot be disadvantaged by the wealth of a private prosecutor, it might be held to be an obvious justice that those who are prosecuted by the State should be defended from the same source; but the position being what it is, and it being in the power of this official to attack any private citizen with all the resources of his department, who must defend himself unaided as best he may, it becomes of some public importance to learn the character and intellectual equipment of the holder of this singular office.

The incidents of the Savidge Enquiry suddenly revealed this gentleman, Sir Archibald Bodkin, to an astonished public, as one who might have been selected in a spirit of impish humour for his supreme unfitness for such an authority. They beheld him as a man of aggressive temperament, of stubborn prejudices, lacking in self-control and in logical faculty. A man who splutters.

After his evidence at that Enquiry, it became the urgent duty of the Government to consider how promptly and publicly he could be removed. The fact that he has been allowed to continue to hold such an appointment shows how little the Home Office appreciates the real cause of the trouble which has arisen, and how completely it is divided from any sympathy with public feeling concerning it.

Sir Archibald Bodkin has exposed himself, to the amazement of his own profession, as well as of the general public, by a formal letter issued over his signature to a firm of solicitors whom he did not credit with ability to estimate it at its proper value, and by evidence given in public on two occasions. .

These events require some detailed consideration. He makes his first appearance in the comedy on May 11, 1928, in this correspondence:

May 11, 1928

My Dear Commissioner,

The 'Money' case as you know has been referred to me by the Home Office. The Secretary of State in the House of Commons mentioned perjury—by the officers—and into this aspect of the matter I wish for some inquiry to be made.

The case has not gone through my registry here—hence my writing to you personally. I should like one of your most experienced C.I.D. officers to be deputed for the matter. Perhaps you would let me know which you propose to select.

Yours sincerely,

A. H. BODKIN

THE POLICE AND THE PUBLIC, BY S. FOWLER WRIGHT

May 11, 1928

My dear Bodkin,

Anderson told me yesterday that he had passed the Money case over to you, and I know it is the wish of everybody concerned that you should investigate it. I am glad. I think the best man we have for the work would be Chief Inspector Collins, and I have told Mr. Wensley to detail him to go and see you as soon as possible.

Yours sincerely,

W. T. HORWOOD

Having already seen something of the mentality of Sir William Horwood, and imagining what his feeling would be toward the agitation which had arisen, we notice with interest that he is 'glad' when he learns that Sir Archibald has been turned loose upon it. He selects Chief Inspector Collins as the most suitable officer to co-operate with him. The responsibility of that selection appears to have rested entirely with Sir William Horwood.

A few days later, Inspector Collins called at the office of the Public Prosecutor, and a long interview took place between them. As to what occurred on that occasion, we have the accounts of both men, and the evidence of the subsequent actions of the Inspector, which partly supports these accounts, though not entirely.

THE POLICE AND THE PUBLIC, BY S. FOWLER WRIGHT

We shall see later what is the general attitude of Sir Archibald towards accused persons, and his ideas of how they should be treated, and it will be curious to compare them with his own account of his instructions to the Inspector. This is what he says, as given in the Majority Report of the Commission, where it is prefaced, and (so to speak) edited in advance by a statement (paragraph eight of the Report), which appears to be intended to justify it. But we will content ourselves with Sir Archibald's own narrative:

> I then told him that the question I was concerned with was whether these two officers, or either of them, had committed perjury in making an absolutely false charge against the two accused persons; that it was a matter of grave importance not only to the public but also to the officers; that at present it appeared that it was a case of oaths against oaths, or, rather, oaths against an oath, as the shorthand notes disclosed that the Magistrate had stopped the case after Sir Leo Money had given evidence and before Miss Savidge was called; and in these circumstances I should want the strictest and most full investigation in order to discover whether there was any counterbalancing fact which would show on the one hand that the officers had committed perjury and the accused were corroborated by such fact in their denials, or whether, on the other hand the officers' stories were true sub-

stantially or entirely. I said it appeared strange that a person of Sir Leo Money's position should be associating with a young woman in a different station of life, and it was essential that I should find out how the acquaintanceship originated, and whether the suggestion made by him at the Police Court that he had been introduced to her by Miss Egan as an employee in a business house with which Sir Leo Money had business relations was or was not true. I wanted to know in what circumstances and how often he had been meeting Miss Savidge; for what purposes; where they went; and what they did. I said it would be necessary to have a full statement from Miss Savidge, Miss Egan, and Sir Leo Money, to begin with. I pointed out that they had been acquitted, and the question now was whether there would be sufficient material to justify me in instituting proceedings for perjury. I also said was necessary to ascertain as to April 23rd how the meeting arose; whether there were any letters in existence from Sir Leo Money to her, or vice versa, and whether there was anything in their attitude or behaviour in Hyde Park which might have given rise to a mistaken suspicion by the officers.

Now the Public Prosecutor was dealing with a case in which accused persons had been tried and acquitted and that case could not properly be reopened under any circumstances. It is true, and it is right to give full weight to this consideration, that a prosecution for perjury against the two officers could not be under taken without the possibility of the circumstances of that acquittal being challenged by the defence, and, to that extent, it might be reasonable, or even necessary for the Public Prosecutor to ascertain that these persons were prepared to support him in the witness-box with unequivocal evidence, and should it have appeared otherwise it might have become his duty to report to the Home Secretary that a prosecution would not be advisable, because the only possible witnesses were unwilling or unable to give him the support he needed.

It might appear to most of us that his first consideration should have been given to the question of whether the evidence as it stood, at its strongest, was sufficient to justify a prosecution for perjury, and, if not, to consider whether the circumstances of the case were such as to make it possible that any further evidence of a reliable kind could be obtainable. It was a case, at its strongest, as he clearly saw, of two against two, and with the possibility of honest mistake in the background. Most of us may think that no prosecution ought to be instituted on the possibility of a jury being persuaded to convict under such circumstances, and the cynical may be inclined to doubt whether such a course were ever seriously contemplated.

If the case, as it stood, were too weak for him properly to ask a jury to convict, and if no further evidence were obtainable, it was waste of time, if nothing worse, to worry those who had already experienced so much annoyance; but if we allow that he may have felt it to be his duty to do so, it is obvious that they should have been approached with a proper courtesy, and with some apology for the further ordeal which he was asking them to consider. This was all the more necessary if he felt it to be his duty to make the offensive suggestion that they might break down in cross-examination, and if he proposed to make a roving enquiry into their previous lives and characters. He must have known that he would be asking them to do that which would be very unwelcome, from which, having already been completely acquitted, they had nothing to gain, and that it was unlikely that they would find compensation in any resentment they might feel against the two constables, or in the abstract pleasure of prosecuting evil-doers in which he is appointed to specialize.

After such direct enquiry, which should have come in the first instance by letter from his office, and not through the medium of a police officer, if it should have appeared that they were willing to give him the assistance which they were under no legal obligation to do, and if he were then in some reasonable doubt as to the stability of the evidence which they would offer, it may be thought (I do not say that I agree), that he would have been justified in spying upon them.

But that was not his procedure at all, and, even accepting his own account of the mental processes from which his words and letters originated, it is obvious that the whole weight of the attack which he instructed the Inspector to deliver was not upon those whose conduct he had been directed to investigate, but upon those who had been already acquitted of the charge against them.

The two constables have had no public opportunity of being heard in their own defence, and I am anxious to avoid any adverse presumption against them, either by word or inference, but I believe—and it was clearly material—that it was demonstrated at the trial that they had given definitely inaccurate evidence (I avoid the suggestion of perjury), as to the locality of the alleged incident. But this does not appear to have interested Sir Archibald. Neither did he suggest the 'detention' of the two constables, which he has said that he regards as the 'common sense' way of dealing with persons against whom a suspicion arises, if there be insufficient evidence to justify their arrest.

Usually, he thinks it would not be in 'the public interest' to be too scrupulous in the methods by which convictions are obtained, but here he has no heart for the chase.

After some days of consideration, we observe that all the details of his instructions are directed against the two acquitted civilians.

He does not speak like a Public Prosecutor, but like a defending counsel. His mind searches for every possible plea which can be set up for the protection of the threatened officers. Is it an 'absolutely' false charge? The Inspector is specially directed to bear in mind that it is a matter of grave importance 'not only to the public, but to the officers', which is obvious enough, but it would be interesting to know whether he is always equally careful to emphasize the feelings of suspected persons when he calls in police assistance in the course of his prosecuting activities.

He does not mention the significance of an experienced magistrate, with the witnesses before him, having dismissed the case without even calling for all the available evidence for the defence, but his mind catches at once upon the point 'it was a case of oaths against oaths, or, rather, of *oaths against an oath*', owing to the second defendant not having been required to deny the accusation.

He instructs the Inspector to make the 'strictest and most full investigation' into the lives and associations of the civilians, but he makes no suggestion of enquiring into the characters or records of the constables in a similar spirit. The latter part of his statement, while ending with a suggestion that there may have been an honest mistake (which is better late than never), contains an implication that is utterly monstrous. It amounts to a proposition that, if any two people are in a public park, and if there be anything in the private lives of either of them, in their mutual relations, or with others, which is discreditable, or which they would object to discuss in public, they must therefore be held to be guilty of acts of public indecency, should such accusation be made against them.

Which is absurd.

Acting on these instructions, Chief Inspector Collins, after discussing the matter with his superior officers, commenced by interviewing the constables whose conduct was the nominal subject of the enquiry. We are not told whether he cautioned them, or whether he took two of the voluntary statements in which he specializes. We are not even told whether he questioned them separately. It appears more probable that he simply fortified himself with their account of the matter before he turned his attention to the serious business of the enquiry which he had been directed to undertake.

THE POLICE AND THE PUBLIC, BY S. FOWLER WRIGHT

In the prosecution of this enterprise, after obtaining the statement from Miss Savidge which we have already considered, he approached the solicitors to Sir Leo Money with a view to obtaining some similar, or other, information from him, and it appears—and is scarcely surprising—that a difference arose as to the subjects with which such a statement should deal, or the conditions under which it should be taken, or both.

It does not appear that these solicitors declined to assist the Public Prosecutor, but they considered (with which most people will agree), that the questions which it was desired to ask should be properly formulated, and receive considered written replies. Inspector Collins resented this method of obtaining statements, and communicated his dissatisfaction to Sir Archibald Bodkin, who came to his support in no uncertain way.

Sir Archibald is a verbose man, and I grudge the space which is required to reproduce his letter, but it seems the fairest method, and I give it in full.

17th May, 1928

Sirs,

re Sir Leo C. Money

I have today received a report from Chief Inspector Collins, New Scotland Yard, of a telephone conversation you had with him yesterday evening about 6 P.M. and, personally, this morning about 11 A.M., from the statements in which it is quite clear that you do not appreciate the position of that officer or the nature of his duties, in desiring to take a full and complete statement from your client, Sir Leo Money, as to the offence with which he was recently charged at the Marlborough Street Police Court, in conjunction with Miss Irene Savidge, and subsequently discharged, the case being dismissed on the 2nd instant on the ground that the learned Magistrate had come to the conclusion that the defendants were not guilty. You are, of course, aware that certain questions were put to the Secretary of State by several Members of Parliament upon this case, and that the Secretary of State announced that amongst other questions was that of whether the two police officers, who gave evidence against your client of the details of the offence, had or had not committed wilful and corrupt perjury, and that later the Secretary of State announced that he had remitted the papers in reference to the question of perjury to the proper authority for consideration—referring to myself as Director of Public Prosecutions. In view of the public importance of the case, not only as affecting your client, but the public generally and the police officers concerned, I determined that there should be a full and complete investigation with a view to obtain, if any existed, satisfactory evidence upon which proceedings for perjury might be instituted. It must be obvious to you that the two principal witnesses, in support of any such charge, would be Sir Leo Money and Miss Savidge, and, accordingly, I adopted what you may, or may not, be aware, is the ordinary course of obtaining for the purpose of making complete investigation the services of as experienced an officer in the Metropolitan Police as was available, and on a personal application to the Commissioner for an officer of experience, Chief Inspector Collins was deputed to take my instructions. I thereupon gave him precise and detailed instructions to take a full statement from Miss Savidge as to the circumstances of her acquaintance with your client—Sir Leo Money—from the time when she first, as is alleged, through another young lady named Miss Egan, became acquainted with him, Miss Savidge, in the circumstances well known to you, not having given any evidence on oath at the Police Court, and this was done on the 15th instant with the full consent of Miss Savidge herself. Referring to your conversation at 6 yesterday, the 16th instant, as reported by Chief Inspector Collins, whom you appear to have reprimanded for having committed some more or less grave irregularity in seeing and taking a statement from Miss Savidge 'without your consent,' I beg to inform you that where I am inquiring into a matter of public concern, such as the possibility of a charge of perjury committed in a matter of which your clients have seriously complained, there is no necessity for me to obtain your consent or, indeed, to consult you in any manner whatsoever, and, if you had taken any steps to prevent Miss Savidge being interviewed, you would have been acting in obstruction of the duty which the reference of this case by the Secretary of State to me has imposed upon me, an attitude which, I am sure, Solicitors, or officers of the Court would be the last to adopt. I gather from the report of Chief Inspector Collins that, having made an appointment to meet Sir Leo Money at your office this morning, and on your being informed that he was acting on my behalf and desired to take a full and complete statement from your client so as to form part of the material which I require to determine whether a charge of perjury shall or shall not be made against those officers, you informed him that you did not and never had complained of perjury and that you had received the advice of Counsel that as the case had been investigated by the Magistrate there was 'no necessity for Sir Leo Money to be subjected to another examination on the same matter.' I confess to feeling some surprise that you should take up this position, considering that your client has been described as a public man, at one time a

Member of Parliament, and his character grievously affected by a charge, the falsity of which might become the subject of a prosecution for perjury. I should have supposed that of all people, Sir Leo Money would have been anxious to assist me by giving, without hesitation, a complete and frank statement of his relations with Miss Savidge, from their commencement until the dismissal of the charge, as well as a statement as to the incidents of the night of the 23rd April.

You must please understand that in my opinion it is obviously essential that I should have full information from Sir Leo for the simple reason that without it I am unable to perform the duty which has been placed upon me, and I must look to you to put no obstacle in my way. The issue involved in any charge of perjury is different in character to the issue which the learned Magistrate had to determine, and the material relevant to that issue of perjury is not to be limited to the occurrences, or alleged occurrences, of the 23rd April. I observe that you repeated more than once to Chief Inspector Collins that you were making no allegations of perjury against the officers and that the case having concluded as it did, Sir Leo Money had no further interest in it. This does not satisfy me—either the officers were speaking the truth or they were testifying to what they must have known was untrue. It is in the interests of the public that I should have material which would enable me to determine what is the proper view to take of officers who are acting as police officers in public places, no matter what the personal feelings of your client or yourselves may be. I must insist upon Sir Leo Money sparing a little of his time to give to the officer acting for me full information upon such matters as I think are material for me to consider. Your suggestion that I should prepare a series of interrogatories which are to be submitted to you, and which Sir Leo Money on your advice, or without it, is either to agree to answer or to refuse to answer, is a wholly impossible proposition, and a moment's reflection, with your experience as Solicitors, will lead you to the same conclusion. It is absolutely and practically impossible to take a statement from a person in any such manner which could be of any use in dealing with a criminal case—with the investigation into which I am not without some familiarity.

The question, therefore, is a very simple one: Will you be good enough, at the earliest possible opportunity, to arrange that Sir Leo Money shall be seen, either at his house, or your office, or at New Scotland Yard, by Chief Inspector Collins, and there and then give a full and frank and detailed narrative upon the matters which I have instructed

THE POLICE AND THE PUBLIC, BY S. FOWLER WRIGHT

Chief Inspector Collins to question him. If you will do so, you and your client will have the advantage of knowing that you are assisting the course of justice, but if you decline I must take other steps to procure what is essential for me to have before me.

I am, Sir, Your obedient Servant

A. H. BODKIN

Messrs. Syrett & Sons
115, Moorgate, E.C. 2

This letter is beyond reasonable defence, and I do not think anyone, unless it be Sir Archibald himself, has attempted to defend it. The Majority Report passes it with a significant absence of comment. The best service it can render to the Public Prosecutor is to avoid him as widely as possible. Mr Lees-Smith, with careful moderation, characterizes it as 'couched in terms unsuitable to the correspondence of a public department'. In plain analysis it is improper in tone, petulant and bullying; illogical in substance; and illegal in its concluding threat; and the more it is considered, the more intolerable it appears that the man who could dictate it should be continued in the office he has degraded.

It would be an insult to any reader's intelligence to discuss at length whether the character of any man should be 'grievously affected' by being acquitted on a false charge; or that persons so acquitted should be logically required, or should become automatically anxious, to answer any questions regarding their mutual relations, or their past lives, which it might occur to a Police Inspector to ask them.

The objection to the presence of their solicitors, or to their giving written replies to written questions, is a sufficient comment on the stubborn assertion by the police that cross-examination does not take place when such statements are obtained by their own methods.

The concluding threat is capable of two interpretations. Sir Archibald either intended to intimidate Sir Leo Money into entering the same trap to which Miss Savidge had fallen by the fear that he might be legally coerced should he continue to refuse, or he meant that he proposed to obtain his ends by subterranean spying, and it is difficult to decide which interpretation condemns him the more completely.

There is another consideration. Sir Archibald had already realized (as anyone would), that even if a charge of perjury could be successful in such a case under any circumstances, it certainly could not be so if the evidence of those concerned should be reluctant or unsatisfactory. If, therefore, as his letter indicates (however illogically), he regarded the attitude of Sir Leo Money as recalcitrant, he must have abandoned the idea of prosecuting the constables (if he ever entertained it), and the letter, both in tone and substance, supports the view that the reference of the case to him by the Home Secretary was regarded, both at Scotland Yard and in his own office, simply and entirely as an opportunity for obtaining evidence, if possible, in the interests of the police, that the accused persons should not have been acquitted at all.

Being called to give evidence before the Savidge Tribunal, Sir Archibald had an opportunity, after reflexion, of expressing his regret for having issued this letter, and his realization of its impropriety.

It would be needless cruelty to go over that evidence in detail, and to observe him in the witness-box plunging clumsily like a tormented bull, but these two replies will be sufficient to show his considered attitude to the impropriety which he had committed.

Mr. Lees-Smith asked him whether he could justify having written that he 'must insist' on Sir Leo Money sparing a little of his time, to which he replied;

> That was an unfortunate word. What I meant was that I must *insist on asking.*
> Mr. Lees-Smith—Do you think that this was a proper letter to have written?
> Sir A. Bodkin—Certainly.

of which it is sufficient to say that the first answer is an...inexactitude, and the second is final evidence of his unfitness for the office he holds.

We now come to Sir Archibald's appearance before the Police Commission, when he revealed himself as a wholehearted advocate for police methods, and gave the impression that, if the decision should rest with him, such private liberties as remain among us would be very quickly ended.

It will be sufficient to make three abstracts from his evidence on this occasion.

He had used, in illustration, the case of a Mrs. Jones, whose husband had died under suspicious circumstances, and who had been 'invited', not to Scotland Yard, but to his own Department, where a statement was taken from her; another person, whom the statement inclined to implicate, being subsequently convicted of murder, and hanged. He mentioned that the statement had taken a long time to obtain.

> The Chairman—Was that cross-examination continuous?
>
> Sir Archibald Bodkin—There was no cross-examination. She was questioned continuously, and her statement prepared, with intervals for lunch and tea, from eleven o'clock in the morning until about 10:30 at night.

Now Sir Archibald Bodkin, whatever may be his mental deficiencies, is an experienced lawyer. He knows what cross-examination is; he knows its purpose and methods; and when he says that Mrs. Jones was questioned 'continuously' for even eight or ten hour and was not cross-examined, he knows that he is talking nonsense.

But the objection to a cross-examination being conducted without the presence of an impartial judge or legal assistance is so obvious that, like Sir William Horwood, he shies at the word, or it might be fairer to say that while Sir William shies, Sir Archibald puts his head down and charges. Sir William declines to 'admit' or 'agree', but Sir Archibald tosses back the suggestion with a blank denial.

Our second quotation relates to what are known as the 'Judges' Rules'—certain regulations prepared some years ago, at the request of the Home Office, for the guidance of those taking statements, or questioning prisoners, having no legal authority, but being of importance as embodying the opinions of judicial minds, and as having been in general use for the guidance of police officers since they were formulated.

It was natural that a Commission engaged in investigation of police powers and procedure should desire the evidence of competent witnesses as to whether these rules are generally observed, whether they have been satisfactory in practice, and what alterations or additions, if any, they can suggest.

No other witness appears to have realized the impropriety of this question, but when it is addressed to Sir Archibald Bodkin, he replies

'As this question seems to me to involve criticism of the Rules I must respectfully decline to answer it.'

Reading this pathetic reply, it is impossible not to feel some sympathy for a man placed by the malice of circumstance in a position for which he is temperamentally unfitted. Nature intended him to be the butler of a Conservative peer. It was a jest of fate that he should be called before a tribunal which invited him at one moment to consider the rights of prisoners, and at the next to criticize the Judges' Rules. Very respectfully, he excused himself from so doing. There was a flavour of impropriety in the suggestion. He knew his respectful duty to the Commission, but no one would induce him to criticize his betters. The butler had been asked to sit down in the drawing room, and very respectfully he declined to do so. As to prisoners, they should know their place, as he knew his.

The third abstract which I am selecting from the Public Prosecutor's evidence must do him more, not less, than justice, owing to its brevity, for we have given him space enough, and to chase his replies to any affirmative thought is to wade in a sea of words and net nothing better than some very flourishing prejudices.

The chairman of the Royal Commission is questioning him on the practice of arresting men on a charge other than that on which it is intended to proceed against them—

> Lord Lee—Is it the custom if an individual is strongly suspected of a grave crime to charge him with a lesser crime in order that you may have a better opportunity of questioning him?
>
> Sir Reginald Poole—Or to get him under lock and key?
>
> Sir Archibald—I should think there are cases in which the police may suspect a certain person, and if they find he has committed some other crime, it is their duty to arrest him and charge him with it. I think from the point of view of the public it is a first-rate procedure.
>
> Lord Lee—We are not questioning whether it is first rate or the reverse, but we are trying to get the facts.

The Police and the Public, by S. Fowler Wright

> Sir Howard Frank—Surely this means that you use a minor charge in order to get round Lord Brampton's rule?
>
> Sir Archibald—No, that is not so.

I have selected this as showing how, the various members of the Commission joined in the Chairman's efforts to abstract ideas which were not there (notice the four questions and the two replies), and how he first evades the issue with an aspect of stupidity, which even in him cannot be quite genuine, and then, being pressed too hard, takes refuge in a denial which places his veracity in opposition to his intelligence, so that the more we rely upon the one, the more we must abandon belief in the other.

It can scarcely need to be pointed out that it has not been suggested by anyone that the police should not arrest any man for a crime of which they have proof, simply because they suspect him of another, of which they have none. The point is in the use to which the arrest is put to entrap him into admissions that may enable them to make a case against him on the second charge; the doubt whether the charge on which he is first arrested or detained (and which may never be tried at all), is always genuine; and the fact that there have been cases in which it has subsequently appeared that the police *had* sufficient evidence to have arrested on the major charge in the first instance, and in which the minor charge seems to have been deliberately selected as a means of bringing pressure or cajolery to secure the 'voluntary statement' required to complete the case on the more serious issue.

The Police and the Public, by S. Fowler Wright

Studying Sir Archibald's reply carefully, it is difficult to understand what he means by the 'first-rate procedure', unless he be endorsing these methods, in the very act of denying or obscuring their use.

It gives us some further illumination of the type of mind and logical faculties of the Public Prosecutor to observe that in reply to the various members of the Commission—all of whom seem to have been roused to interrogation by the quaint evasiveness of the replies which their colleagues obtained—or in written replies to the preliminary questions he received, he stated that he considers that the methods by which the Criminal Investigation Department in the Metropolitan area take statements and pursue enquiries are 'admirable'; that the protection of an accused person against improper questioning is that it could be brought up at the trial; that if it be so brought up, neither court nor jury will pay much attention to it; that when the police arrest a man and do not wish to obey the law, which requires them to bring him before a magistrate immediately, it is a 'common-sense' method to 'detain' him without making any charge at all; that there is no statute or other law to support this practice, but that it is legal if done for three days, and illegal if done for four; that charges against policemen should be investigated by other policemen, because it has been the practice for seventy or eighty years; and that police are less likely to shield one another than servant-girls because (apparently) there must be more *esprit de corps* between 'three heterogeneous items of female society' than in 'a trained and disciplined body'.

THE POLICE AND THE PUBLIC, BY S. FOWLER WRIGHT

I apologize to Sir Archibald if I have misinterpreted the weirdness of the concluding statement, but I have tried to find *some* meaning, and can do no better.

But in reviewing his evidence, though it is remarkable how seldom he answers a question (if at all), at the first attempt, I am inclined to doubt whether he always intends to be as evasive as he appears. He has, very obviously, a mind which objects to be disturbed by thought. To the 'Why?' of his inquisitors he retorts, 'Why not?'—a form of reply making no excessive claims on the intellect.

There being no apparent method of proving that statements are improperly taken, he asserts the propriety of the procedure with absolute confidence.

There being no apparent method of proving that persons are wrongly convicted under the existing system, he asserts with (I believe) honest confidence that it never happens. And if he says it with honest confidence, all gentlemen (except, perhaps, his betters), will believe it without further argument. Let's go to bed, or play billiards.

CHAPTER IX.

THE STAGING OF MURDER TRIALS

Trials for murder in any country, both because of the gravity of the issue, and the strong light of publicity which will be directed upon them, are the supreme test of the quality of its criminal code, and of the spirit in which it is operated.

In a consideration of our police methods, or criminal procedure, it is natural, therefore, to select them for analysis and illustration.

In doing this, we cannot easily make comparison with the procedure of foreign courts, because we have certain principles which are not common to other countries, and which we may be too ready to assume to be superior.

It is, for instance, the tendency of French procedure to concentrate attention rather upon the criminal than the crime, and, to a less extent, this is the case in the courts of the United States.

Our own procedure tends to direct attention upon the crime rather than the alleged criminal, who is treated with cold impartiality, rather as an exhibit in the case than as having any vital interest in its result.

There are important psychological differences resulting from this variation, some of which may be far from favourable to the accused, and I believe it to be a fact that the proportion of convictions obtained is far higher in this country, under our delusive aspect of impartiality, than in either of the countries mentioned.

Even in Scotland, where the procedure approaches more nearly to ours, there is a radical difference in the fact that they admit a verdict of *Not Proven*, which may often be the only honest one which it is possible to give. Cases which would result in such a verdict in a Scottish court, will be the subject in our own of stubborn battles between contending counsel, resulting in verdicts sometimes of acquittal and sometimes of condemnation, or in a disagreement of the jury, which is usually followed by another trial, the result of which cannot be satisfactory.

It is one of the consequences of our mode of trial that it may almost be accepted as a principle of our criminal law that *the worse the crime, the weaker the evidence on which a conviction can be obtained.*

Deliberate murder—murder in its worst form—is not likely to be committed before an audience. This is more or less true of all forms of serious crime. A burglar does not advertise his programme for the coming week, and a forger may choose a solitary hour for his artistic efforts.

Yet in the routine speech which is made by the prosecuting counsel in the opening of a murder trial it is usual—so monotonously usual that it might be printed in advance, and circulated for general use—to tell the jury that it is not customary for a pre-conceived murder to be committed in public, and that they must be prepared for the evidence which will be offered to be circumstantial only.

That is so obvious that the only reasonable motive for emphasizing it must be to discount in advance the weakness of the evidence which is to be put forward. And, for that purpose, it is too often needed, the evidence which is too frequently offered being such as would not be accepted as relevant in any other legal proceeding, either civil or criminal.

If a man were charged with burglary, it would not be considered evidence against him that his grocer's bill was unpaid, and that there was money in the burgled house which would have been useful to discharge it. Any judge would brush it aside on the ground that if there were any real proof against him it was not required, and if there were none, it was useless.

Yet few murder trials, apart from cases of sudden violence or jealousy, are staged without the time of the imprisoned[4] jury being wasted, and worse than wasted, in hearing long-winded evidence of that character—a practice which was reduced to its ultimate absurdity at the scandalous farce of the Pace trial, when the prosecution solemnly put forward evidence as against Mrs. Pace that her insurance on her husband's life was for a very small amount, *and that she had declined to increase it, when asked to do so.*

---

[4] I often wonder when a jury will be empanelled with sufficient manhood to resist the legal insolence of that imprisonment.

THE POLICE AND THE PUBLIC, BY S. FOWLER WRIGHT

But the Pace trial, with all its tragic absurdity, was an inevitable climax to the tendency of many previous years to prosecute people (and, which is worse, to hang them), on a vague suspicion of poisoning, when, in several cases, there has been nothing but an unreliable medical assertion that anyone has been poisoned at all, and no evidence to connect the accused person with the suggested crime on which anyone ought to hang a dog.

I suppose that the recent habit of constructing a murder charge on the basis of a complicated theory of possibilities, which is first put into the minds of the jury, and then buttressed by details of evidence which have been selected for its support, or which it has been built to admit, is encouraged by, if it does not originate in, the universal reading of detective fiction. It is not at all improbable that judge, counsel, jury, and prisoner alike, are all soaked in this plausible ingenious nonsense, most of which does not rise above the Sherlock Holmes level—amusing, childish puzzles, constructed backwards, and with a spurious aspect of logical stability.

Holmes appeared clever to the careless reader, because he was always right in the end. It would be equally easy to bring each of the tales to a different conclusion on the same facts, and show him as a continual fool.

Several murder trials of recent years have read like one of these tales, and the theory of the prosecutor (theory replacing proof), has been constructed backwards in the same way. There has been an ingenious cobweb of suppositions and 'clues', on which some of the most subtle brains in the police force and the legal profession have been occupied, until they have felt that their professional reputations have been at stake in the successful demonstration of the theory they have constructed.

The legal advisers of persons so accused appear to accept the position as inevitable, and offer a defence which is forensic rather than logical.

The public gets a prolonged entertainment, the lawyers get a great deal of money, partly from public funds, and partly from the unfortunate relatives of the accused, and the individual whom the police have selected for the role of criminal fulfils his allotted part—if the torrent of talk have resulted in a general conviction that he is really a murderer, he is hanged at leisure; if it have resulted in an uneasy doubt as to whether there have been a murder at all, he is reprieved, and sent to penal servitude, to think it over.

The proper logical and legal defence to several murder trials of recent years, which have resulted in the deaths of the accused, would have been to offer no evidence, but to insist on the clear fact that the case was unproved when the prosecution closed it.

This position is made worse by the fact that our law of murder is crudely stupid, both in definition and penalty.

English criminal law is capable of great niceness of discrimination. It can divide dishonesty into a score of crimes of differing seriousness. Even so, it is not content with one penalty for each offence, but provides a scale within which they may be graded to the judge's view of an individual delinquency.

Yet for murder it provides one penalty only, and then loosely groups under that heading a variety of homicidal acts, from the most loathsome to the most venial, or even of mere clumsiness or stupidity, as when the misguided bullet of a would be suicide goes astray with fatal consequences.

The agitation against the death penalty would lose most of its strength if it could only follow the explicit direction of a jury, endorsed by the presiding judge, and the Home Secretary; and under such conditions it might well be a legal punishment for any sufficient crime, so that such a man as he who cut off a child's hands a few months ago, to annoy its mother, could be expeditiously ended.

I have said that the staging of recent murder trials had rendered it reasonable to expect that there would be a culmination in some such tragic burlesque as was supplied by the Pace prosecution.

It was unfortunate that public attention was somewhat misdirected to the proceedings in the coroner's court in this case, because, however scandalous, they were of exceptional character, and it is improbable that any other coroner will act in the same way. The real monstrosity was that the Crown would consent to present such a case, however moderately; and no one was surprised when judge and jury united to stop it.

The judge had previously given the Grand Jury a plain hint to throw out the bill, which it was their evident duty to do. But I was once on a Grand Jury at Warwick (more years ago than I care to count) and I remember what happened in that upstairs room which is best left unwritten, and so....

But the Pace case was not different in kind from half-a-dozen other prosecutions which have had a different ending: it was only in degree. There was an absence of anything approaching proof that the husband of the accused woman had died by swallowing poison at all: and there was not even the usual weakness of evidence as to its administration by the accused, there was simply the utter blank absence of any evidence at all.

The one feature in which it may be hoped that it stands alone, and always will, was the police effort to manufacture or obtain such evidence from her infant children. The fact that they actually put one in the witness-box, who had nothing relevant to say, was not, in itself, surprising: irrelevant witnesses are often put forward to obscure the absence of proof at such trials. But that any policeman should think that his duty lay in such questioning shows the effect of machine-training on a man who may be naturally of decent character. Surely, had it been an actual case of murder, the satisfaction of punishing a criminal would have been dearly bought at such a price. Was it hoped or intended that the child should go through life with the consciousness that it had hanged its mother, by its efforts of uncertain memory concerning past trivialities, to which it could have attached no importance when they occurred?

The process by which the Pace prosecution was developed was almost exactly similar to that of others which have not collapsed in the same way.

The malicious slander to the police-station, too easily credited: the taking of 'statements' from all concerned without any solid basis of accusation to justify such a procedure: the collection of endless trivialities of fact or chatter, to he gone over endlessly in the hope that a few could be selected which could be woven into a theory of guilt. It must be seldom, indeed, that so much patient persistence finds so little out of which ingenuity can construct a crime.

A crime might be discovered, might be reconstructed, might even be proved by such methods once in a hundred times; but it seems unlikely. The percentage of plausible theories of criminality on which a prosecution could be commenced, might, unfortunately, be higher. And the more ingenious the theory, the weaker the initial evidence, the more praise will be given to the detective who can develop such a case until he can make the arrest on which his reputation may be founded.

When the long wait is over, and the jury, agreed last, after hours of doubt and disputation, file back into the box, it is not only the prisoner who listens anxious for the fatal words which will give freedom or death the Inspector who has had charge of the case knows that *'Guilty'* will mean that, within the next few minutes) he may be hearing the Judge's commendation publicly given, to be reported as widely as the case read. The more difficult it has been to connect the prisoner with the crime, the more elaborate the structure of supposition on which the theory of his guilt is founded, the more certain is it that the commendation will be received.

But there will be no public approval, no congratulations on his return to headquarters, should the jury have rejected the case for the prosecution. *Is there a single case on record in which a Judge has congratulated an officer in charge of a case which has resulted in the acquittal of the accused?*

CHAPTER X.

PUBLICITY

The question of the advisability of the enforced or unrestricted publicity of all proceedings either at civil or criminal courts is not as simple as is commonly assumed. The position has radically altered since this publicity was first regarded as a protection of the liberties of the subject. There was no public press at that period making money by selling such a report to all whose cultivated curiosity would incline them to pay for reading it. The present publicity is not confined to those who are personally interested, or who avail themselves of the right to be present, and who would ensure a wider publicity were there any flagrant abuse of the rights or liberties of the sued or prosecuted defendant, or were a plaintiff illegally refused a hearing.

It is a fact that the reports which are now circulated serve a useful purpose in familiarizing the public with the unnumbered possibilities of committing 'offences', through which they must steer their cautious lives as best they may, and of the penalties that they will incur if they give the police the slightest opportunity of 'issuing' a summons against them.

It is probable, also, that these reports have a deterrent influence upon any judges or magistrates who might otherwise be inclined to exaggerate their own personalities, and, in other ways, the reactions of public opinion and discussion may be beneficial (though such influences are expressly silenced until judicial proceedings are completed).

On the other hand, there is, in many minds, morbid dread of this publicity, which inflicts on accused persons (including those who are finally declared innocent), a punishment which is often far beyond anything which their conduct deserves, and deters many, who most need the protection of the law from appealing to it.

This evil is very real, and is too little regarded.

How many people suffering wrong or oppression do not appeal for legal protection when they would quickly do so, if they could anticipate a sympathetic hearing in a kindly privacy? How many timid people served with writ or summons in civil process, pay the claim without contesting amount or legality because they lack courage to face the newspaper reports which would follow a defended action?

The English press (with one notorious exception) is singularly free from any blackmailing practices, yet its present mode of reporting the incidents and results of private litigation is the means of widespread black mail in its subtlest and perhaps its deadliest form.

Its existence has been admitted in connexion with the suppression of detailed divorce reports. It was actually argued by the opponents of this reform that it would have an unfortunate result, as petitions would increase, the fear of publicity being removed—as though such publicity were a suitable deterrent from an appeal to the justice of English law.

It is admitted also in the recent suppression of the names of complainants in cases of alleged blackmail, for which the reason is given that people will not otherwise consent to prosecute. It is to be observed that there is no real consideration for the prosecutor, the arrangement is only made because it is the only method by which such trials can be staged at all. I am not objecting to this practice. It may be nothing less than a first hesitating step in the right direction. But I observe that its impulse is not one of any sympathy for the injured party. Had it been found that black-mailed people would still prosecute, and endure the publicity, I think it is certain that no such procedure would have been allowed.

This is also shown by its illogical partiality. A black-mailed man may be pained and injured by the publication of his name in such a connexion, but so may the alleged blackmailer, and, until convicted, he is legally, and may be actually, an innocent man. It seems an obvious equity, if the name of the accuser be withheld, to withhold the name of the accused also—at least, till the trial is complete, and conviction has resulted. Or the name of the accuser might then be published, should the charge have failed.

The whole question is difficult, but there are many possible alterations of the present law, which are, at least, deserving of some consideration.

THE POLICE AND THE PUBLIC, BY S. FOWLER WRIGHT

The publication of the name of an accused person might be prohibited, *unless with his own consent*, until the action should be concluded, and the result announced.

Or there might be a prohibition of all detailed reports until after the conclusion of a criminal trial. This could rarely, if ever, deflect or hinder the course justice, especially as comment on the proceedings is already prohibited during its progress. The publication of the report of a part-heard case is often injurious and unjust, as it will (most commonly), commence with a speech from the prosecuting counsel, making allegations which may or may not be sustained, and some of which may not be supported by any subsequent evidence. I know that this is against a rule of the bar, but no one can be familiar with civil or criminal trials without being aware that such cases have occurred more than once in recent years.

Another possible course would be to place the copyright of all proceedings in the hands of the court, under such safeguards as would prevent suppression or editing of the reports, the proceeds being the ultimate property of the accused in all cases of acquittal (this would alleviate the great injustice of an innocent man being prosecuted by the State, and having to bear the cost of his defence), or of the injured party to the proceedings, if such there should be, or otherwise of the State.

The evil might be attacked from another angle by rendering an editor liable for damages occasioned by such reports, unless he could show that it was a matter of public importance, the onus of proof resting on him.

The fact that the British press is well-conducted, is generally free from the cruder forms of corruption, and scrupulously fair in intention, does not alter the essential baseness of much of the news-mongering by which it lives.

If I were to overhear an unhappy quarrel between two of my neighbours, which I knew it would be very painful to them to have publicly discussed, and I were then to go from door to door to tell their friends and enemies all about it, the meanness of my occupation would not be relieved by the fact that I asked each of them to give me a penny in return for the tale I told.

The British press (like most of the British pressmen), is too good for some of the occupations which it follows simply because they have become a tradition of newspaper work.

The present conditions under which reports of criminal and civil judicial proceedings are circulated by the press must be regarded therefore as having something less than the stability of a natural law. They do some good, but they do a great deal of evil. They gratify curiosity, at the cost of an amount of human misery which may not be easily realized by those of us who are not naturally susceptible to the surrounding chatter of modern life.

But while they continue, for good or evil, they must result in certain mutualities of obligation between pressmen and policemen which are easily open to abuse, and which are said to have been seriously abused during recent years, specifically in the Metropolitan area.

The police can give (or withhold) valuable information to the press. The press can help the police by circulating descriptions of hunted men, by inserting paragraphs which are designed to trap them, or by delaying publication of that which would warn or aid them. The press can also give an individual officer desired publicity.

Valuable information—good 'copy' of any kind—may be sold to the press for money, or exchanged for less material, but no less coveted, favours. It is difficult to see how this position can be altered, or its natural consequences permanently prevented, while the present freedom of publicity is continued. The press is rich and powerful, and there is a large section of the public which likes to read the kind of news which can be obtained from such sources.

Here again, a copyright control of the proceedings in law courts, of whatever kind, would largely reduce the opportunities for such illicit trafficking. But while the conditions remain, the evil must continue, modified only by the prevailing ethical standards of police and journalistic work.

CHAPTER XI.

Conclusions

Only an English poet could have written

> Order is heav'n's first law (*Essay on Man*, IV. 49)

and been admired for such nonsense.

It was because Alexander Pope was capable of such a delusion that, in spite of his devotion to his art, and his marvellous metrical skill, he is not one of the greatest of English poets.

He had no admiration for the affluent disorders of Nature: no conception of the inevitable consequences of growth and change.

Had he been appointed acting-manager to the Creator, his first operation would have been to straighten the stars. When they had been arranged in a mathematical pattern, he would have felt that he had at least commenced to tidy up the mess in which the Creator worked.

Perhaps, in this, I am saying no more than that he had a finite mind. Order is the necessity of the finite, as disorder is the necessity of the infinite. Disorder is the law of life, and growth, and change. Order is the law of death. There is no change in death.

And this necessity of all finite intelligence, this need of weakness, is particularly strong in the English character, a fact which is not altogether good, nor entirely evil.

The majority of English people will face any adversity, even death itself, without much perturbation, providing they are assured that the proceeding is not unconventional, and is according to use and custom.

They will bury ten-thousand children that have died from measles or scarlet fever, and scarcely notice what they are doing, in the comfortable knowledge that their parents were addicted to the same activity. But if three children should die of bubonic plague, it would be an epidemic. The newspapers would flare into startling headlines. Every mother would look in fear at her children, expecting so prevalent a disease to show its symptoms upon them. They would look at one another in consternation, whispering *'It isn't done'*, in that delightfully self-revealing phase which is the slang of the moment.

There is scarcely an inhabitant of London who would not be appalled and terrified were he told that thirty-thousand of his fellow-citizens had been killed or wounded by burglars last year, and that he must expect his year to show a higher total. Yet he is scarcely interested when he reads that this price of blood is paid for the convenience of the London traffic, because the process of this manslaughter has been orderly, gradual, methodical, with the impetus of a great manufacturing industry behind it. Even if the rush of traffic be swung suddenly in the wrong direction, so that the wariest may feel its wheels go over them, he is not greatly troubled, if it be done with an official formality. He will like to know that the lorry which is destined to pulp him will be impulsed by a Regulation, and that he will be cleared up promptly. *'Let all things be done decently, and in order.'*

But how loud would be the outcry were the entrails of one crushed body left untidily upon the place of its slaughter!

Considering these facts, bureaucratic minds may conclude that the English race is of an invincible docility, and that the only limit to the extent to which it can be abused or exploited is that of their own moderation.

But our history shows conclusively that this is not so.

It may be true that, of all the nations of mankind that have now spread over more than half the land-surface of the earth, those of English blood are the easiest to control.

They have a passion for organization, a love of discipline, a respect for authority, which render even injustice comparatively tolerable, if it be methodically inflicted, and its results may be pre-calculated with some precision.

But if they be driven too hard, if they be ignored too contemptuously, these very qualities make them the more formidable to those who have abused the authority which they had permitted.

The bureaucrat may step more jauntily, observing that the printers of the *New Statesman* have been induced (I wonder how), to purr round Sir William Horwood's ankles on the front page of the *Times*, in deference to the 'high office' which he has very properly vacated.

But that jauntiness would lessen could he understand the reactions of those who read it, who are not on the pay-rolls of the Civil Service.

It is not by such methods that a challenged authority can recruit its strength. Certainly not in this country.

No governing authority is ever likely to fall in England at the hand of its enemies, certainly not to the forces of disorder, which are antipathetic to our national character—unless it have first betrayed itself.

But if the almost exhaustless English patience is strained to the breaking-point by police irritations, the only remedy is to reduce them.

We have seen that while the endless oppression of laws and bylaws, beyond knowledge or number, must be expected to continue, and to increase continually, the most effectual remedy is in the hands of the police themselves, or in the magistrates who should control them. At least nine-tenths of the summonses which are issued at the instigation of the police are public nuisances, vexatious and needless; or are issued with no better object than the collection of revenue-producing fines, which is about the most oppressive form in which taxation can be levied.

While this power is in the hands of the police, and while it is exercised in its present spirit, and is condoned or encouraged by the magistracy, bribery and other forms of corruption are inevitable, and, bad as they are, probably avert more evil than they occasion. They will not be suppressed by severity of punishment, as they are too difficult to detect, and the temptations, on both sides, are greater than is the risk of such detection.

Whatever may be the difficulty of detecting and suppressing certain forms of vice by more open methods (and these difficulties may be exaggerated), there is more loss than gain, even on the lowest ground of expediency, in instigating or allowing policemen to disguise themselves for penetration or participation in the illegalities they are to report for prosecution.

For a policeman to accept bribes from these vice mongers is about the lowest degradation to which he can descend (a policeman who accepts half-a-crown not to 're-port' a man who has accidentally left his driving-license in another coat, is not to be seriously compared with one who accepts a bribe to condone the practices of the road-hog or the prostitute-farmer), but if a class of men be selected for such work who are prepared to spy and lie to the order of their superiors, is it not likely that they will betray both sides in turn when it is so profitable to do so?

So far as corruption can be eliminated, it is by training the new recruits in self-respect and honour, letting them feel that the police-force is organized for, and not against, the public, praising and promoting them for keeping order and good-feeling in their beats and districts without report of friction, rather than for the arrests they make, or the irregularities which they report for prosecution.

One of the witnesses before the Royal Commission remarked with emphasis that it is the duty of the police to detect crime as well as to prevent it. That is true, though it would be well to reverse the emphasis.

THE POLICE AND THE PUBLIC, BY S. FOWLER WRIGHT

The detection and punishment of crime is their inferior, and should be their more distasteful work. It is important. It is sometimes dangerous. It demands many admirable qualities both of mind and body. It should have the active sympathy and support of every citizen of good character. There have been complaints from the police that such support is sometimes reluctant or refused. If this be so, must it not be evidence of the evil which I have tried to probe, and for which I suggest a remedy? Even the conviction of a criminal may be bought too dearly.

Let the police purge from their pursuit of crime methods which suggest that they regard it as a lawless sport. Let it appear that they regard it as their part in the complex life of the community to explain and regulate, rather than to vex with unending prosecutions; let their own methods be simple and honourable; and few who are familiar with English character will doubt that they will, as a force, be as popular as most of them, individually, already are; or that they will gain the ready help of thousands who now look upon a police-station with disfavour, and the visit of a police officer with an inward fear.

The police-force, even as at present operated, does not deserve the full measure of the discredit to which it has fallen. Detective Quinlan, who recently arrested a man for theft in Marylebone, and then went to purchase food for his children, is no exception to the spirit animating thousands of his fellow-officers, who may not be likely to be brought into public view. Years ago, I came into personal contact with a similar incident, and I have no doubt that they are numerous.

As a whole, it is a force in which kindliness and courage are equally and entirely common.

If the object of the Government, in regard to the Savidge Enquiry, and other matters, has been to increase the popularity of the police, its purpose has been good, but its method futile.

It was a case in which frankness and open exercise of discipline was the wisest, as well as the most courageous course.

But the taint of war-time methods is still with us, and is not only illustrated by the taking of statements. Bureaucracy fears the light, and the politicians have not sufficient imagination to understand that, if they would trust those on whom their elections depend, they could afford to defy it.

If I have criticized the spirit in which the Government has faced this problem, it has not been from any party bias. I do not suggest that a Socialist Government would have done better, or differently.

It is quite likely that the Government we have is better than any likely substitute. A Socialist one might lead us to many follies, and some disasters. But the more we realize that possibility, the more must we be inclined to protest when we see it throw away its opportunities of popularity. It is not enough for it to rely upon the fact that it plies the financial whips so heartily that we are unlikely to vote for its opponents' scorpions.

The English people may be the easiest in the world to drive, but they hate to be driven in blinkers. Almost equally, they hate to feel a weak hand on the rein.

The Police and the Public, by S. Fowler Wright

It is true of any English government that if it cannot lead with courage, it will be rejected with ignominy.

It is because politicians cannot accept this fact that our governments change so frequently.

Mr. Lloyd George showed a flicker of courage during the war, and he became immensely popular. Afterwards, he declared his intention of hanging the Kaiser, and though no one particularly desired or expected such an event, it was a gesture of pugnacity which secured his triumphant return to power. Then he temporised and vacillated before the problems of peace, and he was thrown aside.

The popularity of Mr. Stanley Baldwin today, lessened though it may be by his unwillingness to discipline colleagues of inferior ability to himself, is still firmly based upon the courage which he showed in risking his political future for an unpopular policy.

If Mussolini could stand tomorrow for any constituency in England, he would be elected by an overwhelming majority, and the reason is in the fact that had he been at the head of the English government the Majority Report of the Savidge Commission would not exist, for neither Sir John Eldon Bankes, nor any other man, would have dared to present him with such a document.

ABOUT THE AUTHOR

SYDNEY FOWLER WRIGHT (1874-1965) penned over seventy volumes of science fiction, fantasy, classic mysteries, historical novels, poetry, and non-fiction, many of them being published by the Borgo Press Imprint of Wildside Press.

www.ingramcontent.com/pod-product-compliance
Ingram Content Group UK Ltd.
Pitfield, Milton Keynes, MK11 3LW, UK
UKHW041436180426
11947UKWH00007B/479